MORE THAN LAUGHTER

My Days on the Tonight Show

Starring

JOHNNY CARSON

by

Sy Kasoff

ISBN# 1-58721-085-1

This book is printed on acid free paper

1stbooks – rev. 9/05/01

MORE THAN LAUGHTER

My Days on the Tonight Show

Starring

JOHNNY CARSON

For Harold and Phyllis T.

And a dozen or so other players.

Good friends, all.

AUTHOR'S NOTE

This book tells of my adventures on the *Tonight Show* and speaks to my particular take on Johnny, who, as a talk show host, was an anomaly from the start -- too private a person (too shy, actually) to ever be comfortable in the one-on-one exchanges that are the mainsprings of the talk show game. Yet, he succeeded beyond anyone's expectations, parlaying a quick and engaging wit with a kind of Everyman sensibility, holding up a mirror to his audience through which they saw, ten times over, refracted images of themselves. It was all a bit of magic, actually, as happens sometimes, the parties winding up practically in cahoots with one another.

This perception, whatever its merits, came to me pretty much *after* I left the show. But while I was there, even without ever fully comprehending the why of Johnny's success, I had a very good time.

I GOT A CALL ONE DAY FROM AN UNEXPECTED source, a woman in the PR department of the University of Michigan. She told me that the Michigan professor who had come up with the then-new science of cryonics (his term) -- the freezing of a body at the instant of death, and unfreezing it, once a cure had been found for whatever had caused the fatal illness -- would be coming to New York in the near future. Might we be interested in him as a guest on the *Tonight Show*?

Indeed, we might. Properly handled, the spot could be a winner.

She said he was going to be in Manhattan for only one night and would not want to spend any more time in the Big Apple than was absolutely necessary.

I put her on hold, buzzed Art Stark, the show's producer, and walked it by him. Without hesitating, he said the magic words:

"Book him!"

There was a problem, however.

Zsa-Zsa Gabor had already been scheduled for an appearance on the same night. (We taped at 6:30PM, straight through, as if it were a "live" show.) A great beauty, Zsa-Zsa was well-known for making outrageous remarks, even after she had been moved from the swivel chair to the couch, and was likely to disrupt any discussion of a subject that called for a semblance of restraint, let alone flat-out good taste.

We could move her to another night, or try to, but she might take umbrage; in those days it seemed she was practically looking for opportunities to draw public attention to herself.

If we did move her, we'd have to come up with a replacement, and in a hurry. And finding good women guests -- to grace the panel, if nothing else -- was an ongoing problem. *And*, we still had to book the all-important third guest -- actually, the *second* guest, the professor being the "third" guest, the one who would come on the show during its last half-hour. It ran for an hour-and-a-half, in those days, until 1:00 A.M.

Art Stark's policy, at the time, was to have another comedian on every night, to give Johnny a little support, make him feel comfortable. For us talent coordinators, the task was clear: find someone who was mature enough to refrain from making tasteless jokes, at what was bound to be a big fat target -- death and dying, and freezing and thawing -- while being able, as well, to help keep Zsa-Zsa at bay.

Alan King, the sanest of all the comics, was everybody's first choice.

But an unexpected thing happened when it all came together.

Alan, evidently deeply offended by the whole idea of tampering with the life cycle's natural order, surprised us all by trashing the teacher. But Zsa-Zsa, to everyone's even greater surprise, saved the day. She asked thoughtful and probing questions, clearly very interested in the whole procedure.

Well, of course she was; she didn't want to go, ever. But if she had to, think of the reception she'd get when she came back!

2

The way it worked out was totally unexpected, and a little hairy, but ultimately great fun. Had we been as smart as we thought we were, we could have anticipated it. *Should've* anticipated it.

Maybe not.

I JOINED THE STAFF OF THE *TONIGHT SHOW* in August, 1962, five or six weeks before Johnny took over as its new host.

Before that, I'd been working on another talk show -- *PM*, hosted by Mike Wallace -- as a general assistant, a job I got only because the guy who hired me inexplicably assumed that, because I had had some experience in promoting a television viewing audience, I would be able to get a *studio* audience, which they were having trouble attracting, to watch the show being taped.

Soon enough, they had to hire a specialist to do the job. Buddy Piper, an amiable chap, employed young people to stand on busy street corners and hand out tickets to various shows, the number to be distributed determined by an arithmetic formula of Buddy's own devising. "It's what I do," he told me solemnly, when we met -- the first time I ever heard anyone characterize himself in that way.

By golly, he did get us a studio audience.

That left me answering fan mail and leading the applause during tapings. Why they kept me on, I'll never know. Why I stayed on is easier to answer: I simply couldn't afford to leave.

All the while, it was becoming increasingly clear that the show was in a lot of trouble.

Though extremely well executed, its ratings, in most markets up against the mighty *Tonight Show*, were weak; as a consequence, few "quality" guests were clamoring to come on board.

My own unyielding discontent, and the fact that Mert Koplin, *PM's* producer, was one of the sweetest guys in the business, gave me the temerity to present the man who had hired me, the executive producer, with an ultimatum: Give me a shot at booking talent -- something I'd never done before -- or I'm outta here.

It was ridiculous, of course. Who cared if I quit? Or stayed, for that matter. But the show had only one talent coordinator. With me, they would have a second -- on the cheap. If I didn't work out, *then* they could fire me.

Mert Koplin backed me up, and I got the job.

The present booker was pointedly uncommunicative. He assured me that I shouldn't worry, I'd pick things up as I went along.

Although I already knew about agents and managers and public relations people, I hadn't yet made the connection between the roles they played and the process of booking guests.

Thus, when I read, on maybe my second or third day, that Burt Lancaster -- then a major, major motion picture star -- was in New York, at the Plaza hotel, here to promote his new movie, *Birdman of Alcatraz*, I picked up the phone and dialed him direct. Not unexpectedly, someone other than Lancaster answered the phone. I introduced myself and told whoever it was why I was calling.

"Hold on a minute," he said. I could hear him, his face turned away from the phone, calling out: "Hey, Burt. They want you to do *PM*. You know, Mike Wallace . . . . "

He went off the line, but, remarkably, soon returned.

"When do you want him?"

I couldn't believe it.

"Great!" I said. "Let me check with the producer. I'll get back to you in ten minutes . . . "

I hung up and sprinted down the hallway, to Mert's office. Fortunately, he was there, together with a few of the other production people, and, as it happens, the Executive Producer.

"I got Burt Lancaster!" I proclaimed.

Everyone turned in my direction. Mert, smiling, raised an eyebrow. "Are you sure?"

"Absolutely."

There was a quick discussion, and a date for Lancaster's appearance was chosen. I called the Plaza, straightaway, and locked it in.

On the appointed day, at the final production meeting, I was surprised and disheartened to hear Mert say to Mike: "So, we're doing a *Nightbeat* interview with Burt, right?" Already, they were on a first-name basis with the star, a commonplace in the business.

"Well, yes," Mike said. "Isn't that what we agreed to do?"

Nightbeat was a show Wallace had done in the earliest days of television: he and a guest, on stools, the set in darkness, except for pools of light on the two players, with Mike routinely asking questions of a highly personal nature. On one of them, he had talked "openly" to Tennessee Williams about Williams's homosexuality -- very much a taboo topic, at the time -- the camera tight on the playwright's face, his terrible discomfort for all to see. Kim Novak, a former movie star, had unexpectedly requested

7

such an interview on our show, two weeks earlier. It had gone very well.

But now, they were talking about *springing* it on the only really heavyweight guest *PM* had ever had, despite knowing full well the implicit terms of any booking: the guest gets to plug his movie (or whatever), while the show gets the benefit of his marquee value -- as well as the pleasure of his company.

I didn't get it. What was it with these people? Didn't they realize how wrong this was? How stupid? I raised my hand and said, "He's coming on to talk about his movie, *Birdman* . . . " but the meeting was already breaking up. I left the room, disheartened.

The taping was a disaster.

It started off nicely enough. A few minutes of friendly chitchat, some smiles and laughter, a glancing reference by Mike to *Birdman of Alcatraz*. Lancaster, looking even better in person than on the screen, was charming and gracious: good company. He had great presence, a man clearly at one with himself, and seemed to be having a good time.

Until his host started up.

Some people, Wallace said, were making certain allegations about Lancaster's private life. He hinted at their content. "Are they true?" he asked.

Lancaster studied his host for a long moment. Speaking in a lowered voice, he stated that he never responded to that kind of question. Indeed, he was rather surprised to hear it coming from someone of Mike Wallace's stature. He was smiling, but there was menace in it. The message was clear: Let's get on with it, shall we? We'll let this one pass . . .

Mike didn't get it. In fact, he looked as if he had scored an important point. If Lancaster had done nothing wrong, why hadn't he said so?

And how about the actor's virtual cameo appearance in *Judgement At Nuremberg*?

"You were paid $900,000" -- no small sum, in those days -- "for what amounted to only seven minutes on the screen. How can you justify earning so much money for so little work?" Mike tried to make it appear that he was just being offhandedly curious, but he fooled no one, least of all Lancaster. The two weren't on stools, as on *Nightbeat*, spotlighted in the dark, but they might as well have been.

The movie star took a deep breath and with exaggerated patience explained that others, in fact, were responsible for the length of time he was on the screen, not he.

More important, the value of an actor's performance, his worth to a film, could not be measured with a stopwatch. It was more complicated than that, ran deeper.

"As I'm sure you know, Mr. Wallace."

Undaunted, undeterred -- God knows what he was thinking -- Mike came up with another question of the same order and in the same judgmental tone. And another. Lancaster pretty much ignored or deflected both. He looked increasingly perturbed. Mike either didn't notice, or chose not to, the while rigorously maintaining an air of reasonableness and calm.

"Mr. Lancaster," he began again, "what I don't understand is --"

But this time "Burt" overrode him.

"Mr. Wallace!" he snapped. "What *I* don't understand is that I came here to talk about a motion picture that means a lot to me, one I've worked on long and hard. Very hard. And now you give me this?? An *interrogation!*"

Mike's eyes widened.

Lancaster stared at him.

"I tell you, sir," he declared, extremely agitated and looking very dangerous, "I've never encountered anything so unprofessional in my life!" Abruptly, he rose from his chair and leaned into his host. Holding the pose, giving the moment its due.

"You asshole!" he muttered, finally.

Then, moving like a panther, he strode off the set and left the studio, *Birdman's* PR guy scrambling to keep up. Out of there!

Mike was stunned, unable to comprehend what had just happened. How? Why? It took Mert Koplin, who had stopped tape upon Lancaster's exit, a full twenty minutes to settle *his* star down.

My take on the whole wretched business was that Wallace was the prime mover in pulling the switch on Lancaster. The prospect of taking the measure of such a major celebrity was just too much for him to resist. Hit a home run and save the show, so what if your guest is made a little uncomfortable. Demonstrating his well-known hectoring skills early on.

Unfortunately, it didn't work out as planned, insofar as there had been any real planning involved. Still, all the publicity the event was bound to stir up, might, in itself, make a difference. Enough to . . . -- well, it *could* happen.

The next day, Lancaster's walking off the set was, indeed, the buzz all over town. All five New York newspapers featured the story prominently, three on the front page, with pictures. It didn't help. A couple of weeks later, *PM* was no more. Just about the entire staff hied over to the *Tonight Show* offices, looking for work. They were all overqualified for the one position available: talent coordinator. On my resume, it said I had been doing it for six months. I was hired on the spot.

Why the *Tonight Show* had not gone after Burt, or why he hadn't been offered to them in the first place, I have no idea.

THE MAN WHO HIRED ME WAS PERRY CROSS, the *Tonight Show's* producer, at the time.

He told me that his talent coordinators not only booked the show -- well, actually, *he* did the booking -- but, unlike *PM*, pre-interviewed their guests, as well.

"Sit in with Bob Shanks for a couple of days," he said. "You'll pick it up in no time."

Shanks was one of *Tonight's* two associate producers, and its head talent coordinator. "He'll be leaving soon," Cross added, conspiratorially. "When that happens, you'll be taking his place." He shook my hand and smiled disarmingly. "See you Monday. And don't forget your Rolodex!"

I smiled back. How can you forget what you've never had?

This was towards the end of August, 1962.

Jack Paar had quit the show in the spring, and from that point on, guest hosts had taken over, for a week -- sometimes, two -- at a time. Merv Griffin had just completed his first week, and was about to do another. Plans were already in motion for him to have his own talk show -- in syndication, like *PM* was. And Bob Shanks would be producing it.

Jerry Lewis was scheduled to be the next guest host. By the time he came on, Shanks had already left, and I was officially proclaimed Head Talent Coordinator. Right then and there, Perry Cross picked up the phone and told Accounting -- no discussion! -- to add $25 to my salary. That brought it to a stunning $225 a week -- *not* a lot of money, even in those days.

But at that point, what did I care?

I had gone, for no discernible reason, from being almost out of a job to Head Talent Coordinator on the *Tonight Show*, in a matter of weeks. It was heady stuff, and I was more than content to go along for the ride.

LEWIS WAS AT THE TOP OF HIS GAME. EASY, self-assured, thoroughly ingratiating. He charmed us all.

Maturity became him.

As a host he was only mildly off-the-wall. Nothing more outrageous than singing, "Maria! I just met a boy (sic) named Maria . . . " from *West Side Story*. On one of his shows, with only three or four minutes to go, he unexpectedly invited the studio audience to come on stage and dance. A sizeable number of them did, maybe fifty or sixty people. They packed the stage and had a dandy time -- on camera. It looked like the senior prom.

I always got a kick out of Jerry.

He and Dean Martin did a segment on radio, "many moons ago" -- one of Carson's favorite phrases, to which he gave a nasal, Jackie Gleason-style reading -- where the two of them are romancing some gals, Dean making points and Jerry in a world of his own.

Dance music is heard.

"Oh, goody!" Jerry says. "Now, we can do the minuet."

"Jerry," Martin protests, "the minuet went out with the gavotte!"

Lewis (in disbelief): "The gavotte is out?"

Some time during Jerry's two weeks, the Supreme Court arrived at its landmark decision, outlawing mandatory prayer in public schools.

An irate Ed Sullivan -- then, a big star on television -- called Lewis directly and asked to come on the show. Hugh Downs, Jack Paar's announcer, was still with us, having agreed to stay on during the interim period, while waiting to take over as host of the *Today Show*. He and I were quite concerned about the position Sullivan was likely to take. Hugh asked me if I could give him some material on the subject, a paragraph or two, the better to make his case in support of the Court's decision. I said I'd be happy to.

During the taping, show biz veteran George Jessel, the other guest, agreed wholeheartedly with Sullivan. Both were condescending towards anyone who disagreed with them, while Lewis advocated leaving it to the kids to decide. Hugh, bless him, was a welcome voice of sweet reason.

Afterwards, he wondered aloud if I might be interested in joining him on *Today*.

"I don't suppose you'd want to leave the *Tonight Show*, but if you do . . . "

I declined, with thanks. Downs didn't know, of course, that I had only just started and might not be what he apparently thought I was.

A few weeks later, I bumped into him in the men's room, on the seventh floor at "30 Rock." (30 Rockefeller Plaza, the home of NBC.) He told me he had received a letter from George Jessel, in which Jessel apologized for not having examined the issue with more care earlier. Now, he no longer felt as he did then.

Jerry's "overnights" -- spot ratings from the major markets -- were huge, as high as many prime time shows. As a consequence, he got *his* own talk show -- on ABC.

When he left, after his second week, he gave everyone involved in the Tonight Show's production -- some twenty-six people -- a $100 gift certificate to Dunhill's, the swank tobacco shop on Manhattan's Fifth Avenue.

AND NOW, HEEERE'S JOHNNY!

We knew little about him.

He was a comedian from Nebraska who, for the past four years, had hosted a daytime quiz show, taped in New York, called *Who Do You Trust?*

To us he appeared to be somewhat distant, though of an even disposition -- not at all classically temperamental. (He did twitch a tad, at times.) But it soon became clear that he was able to communicate only in the comic mode. When he wasn't pontificating, that is, over something he had just read in *Readers Digest.* And he was surprisingly uninformed about matters of fairly common knowledge.

Furthermore, he was painfully self-conscious. So much so that we felt awkward and uncomfortable in his presence, sensing how awkward and uncomfortable he felt in ours. He silenced any group he came upon.

It was no surprise then that, when doing the show, he demonstrated little capacity for small talk, for the simple give and take of normal, everyday discourse. And since he was virtually unable to initiate matters on his own, every minute of the show would have to be accounted for.

Not an easy situation, for either him or us.

But he was very bright and willing to listen, for much was at stake. Moreover, indisputably and from Day One, he was funny. Very, very funny.

The question was, for a talk-show host, would that be enough?

FOR ED McMAHON AND ME, GETTING together on October 1, 1962 -- Johnny's first day -- was something of a reunion. We had both received our basic training in television at WCAU-TV, a CBS-owned station in Philadelphia, and a wonderful place to work. Ed had been Carson's announcer on his daytime show, as he would be with us. It appeared to be bad casting -- as opposed to say, Jack Paar and Hugh Downs, the one volatile, the other calm and detached.

The fact is, McMahon was not really suited to be anyone's second banana. Quick-thinking, comfortable with people, interested in the world around him, he would have made a first-rate talk show host himself, as he well knew.

To his credit, he played the hand he was dealt with great fidelity, for the most part, providing strong support to Johnny for what turned out to be thirty years. His hearty laugh was genuine and, in cueing the audience, integral to Johnny's success . . . -- certainly, in the early years.

He and I discovered that we shared a common anxiety: food. We were both so preoccupied with it that, while eating breakfast, we were already contemplating -- and worrying about -- what would be on the menu for lunch and dinner, and at what times.

Rather odd, wouldn't you say? Not one such, but two, on the same show?

GEORGE JESSEL AND ED SULLIVAN HAD BEEN on one of Jerry Lewis's shows. They also appeared with Carson -- George (pronounced "Georgie") quite frequently, Sullivan only once. Each made his own particular contribution.

Jessel was a favorite of mine.

In his mid-sixties, I would guess -- "old", in those days -- he had energy that belied his age and a thriving ego, always looking dapper, his back uncommonly straight -- with the assistance of a corset, to be sure, which he would sometimes kid about.

"My girdle is *killing* me!"

As a younger man, Georgie had been a top vaudeville performer, then a movie producer and sometime actor, and, always, a chaser of women, preferably younger women. At some point along the way, he had become a public speaker -- at dinners and celebrity events, with funerals his specialty. To many, he was a ridiculous figure, but I knew better. He had a ready wit, and a generous heart.

One time, he made his entrance to the show, unexpectedly wearing a tuxedo. Johnny took one look, and immediately jumped up, swept his desk clean, and stretched out on his back, eyes closed, arms folded across his chest. When Jessel, prompted by the laughter, caught on, he immediately began to mime a eulogy. With exaggerated gestures.

Jim Fowler, the wild animal guy, was on the same show. He had brought along with him, among other animals, a kinkajou -- a species of monkey.

Johnny asked Jessel if he had ever seen one before. No, Georgie replied, although he had an *uncle* who was a kinky Jew. They shook their heads in tacit agreement: no, it was not the same thing.

On another occasion, Georgie and Richard Tucker, of the Metropolitan Opera, were alone in the Green Room, all made up and ready to go. Standing side by side, they contemplated their images in the mirror. Jessel had brought with him -- not for the first time -- a young woman to see the show. She was already seated prominently in the audience.

He spoke to Tucker in Yiddish.

"*Hosst du gezayne mein maydel*?" Have you seen my girl?

The great tenor allowed that he had.

"*Zayer shane*," he noted, solemnly. Very pretty.

Jessel nodded.

"*Zee iz vee a kind. Voss meer git er, nemtz in moyel.*" She is like a child. Whatever you give her, she puts in her mouth.

Neither of them cracked a smile; I fell apart.

Occasionally, Georgie told jokes on the show.

A woman admires another woman's fabulous ring. A real sparkler.

"It's the Klopman diamond," the other woman says. "It comes with a curse."

"What's the curse?"

"Klopman!"

As he was breaking up, Johnny echoed the punch line -- "Klopman!" -- which, it turned out, he did every time he heard a joke.

The phenomenon was not unfamiliar to me. I had an uncle who used to do that, as well. Twenty years later, so did one of his sons. "I don't know if you guys know it or not," I once pointed out to them, "but when you hear something funny, you both repeat the punch line." "Repeat the punch line," they said, in unison, guffawing.

Ed Sullivan's lone appearance came about as a result of Johnny being named the March Of Dimes "Man Of The Year".

We got the word around three o'clock. Sullivan, along with Broadway columnist, Earl Wilson, and stand-up comic, Joey Adams, wanted to come on the show and let the world in on it. The spot would run in the segment following the monologue, the only place for it, the whole thing to last about four minutes. It would be a surprise.

The only problem -- my problem -- was logistical: getting three people on, and in what order; who would speak first, and say what, etc.

While I was attending to the guest I had pre-interviewed earlier, a simple plan came to mind, emphasis on simple. Ed, a former Broadway columnist, like Wilson, had displayed few performing skills as the host of his own "live" variety show, a longtime TV staple, at 8:00PM on Sunday nights. On the last one I had seen, he was so discombobulated that, at the show's end, he wished everyone a Merry Christmas -- this on the eve of Labor Day!

I went down to the studio at a little before six. Earl and Joey were already there.

I asked them -- as a courtesy, really -- if they had anything in mind. They considered it. Then, Earl said, "Let's wait 'til Ed gets here . . . " and Joey agreed. "Yeah. Let's wait 'til Ed gets here."

At 6:08 P.M., the man himself stepped off the elevator. He was late; we taped at six-thirty. I introduced myself and led him into makeup. He told me we did a great job and whatever we wanted to do was fine with him.

I unfolded my plan.

"You'll come out first, Ed. You'll acknowledge the applause, shake Johnny's hand . . . and Ed McMahon's, if you like. Then, you'll sit in the swivel chair, and say" -- here I unconsciously switched to the way he talked on his own show -- "'Johnny, I've brought along two friends of yours . . . friends of the Tonight Show audience -- Earl Wilson and Joey Adams. Earl, Joey, come out here!'"

Sullivan nodded sagely. He gestured distractedly to the makeup man. "Not too much, fellow. I don't want to look *too* pretty." He laughed.

"They'll come out," I continued, eyeing him in the mirror. "Earl will sit to your right, on the couch, with Joey next to him. Then, you'll say, 'Earl, why don't you tell these good people why we're here.'" I took a deep breath and gazed directly into the TV star's clear blue eyes. "And that's really all you'll have to do, Ed. Okay?"

"You guys do a great job", he said again. "I mean it."

A few minutes later, he came out of makeup and looked around, craning his neck. Spotting me, he beckoned.

"Now, I come out first, then Earl, then Joey, right?"

I staggered, slightly.

"Well, yeah," I said. "We could do it that way, I suppose. But . . . no, let's stay with what we talked about. Okay?"

As we made our way to the green room, I went through it again, Ed waving hello to the many people who hailed him. I then spoke to Earl and Joey.

"Earl, you make the presentation, and Joey, just one joke, please. We don't have the time . . . "

Turning, I almost collided with Sullivan, who was coming out of the green room. He looked exceedingly uncomfortable.

"So, uh, how does it go?" he asked.

Oh, dear.

"Tell you what," I said, as if a new idea had just occurred to me, "let's try it this way . . . " And I went through it again, exactly as before.

The show was about to begin.

During the commercial that followed the monologue, I hastened backstage. Ed was clearly in distress. For the last time, I laid it out for him, talking as if to a Bar Mitzvah boy -- he, one of the major players in the business. On the TV monitor, Johnny was at his desk, McMahon in the swivel chair. I cued Sullivan out.

The audience gasped and applauded enthusiastically at Ed's unexpected appearance. Johnny was properly "surprised" and accepted the award graciously, while Sullivan followed the "script" pretty much word for word.

In his only ad lib, he poked fun at himself, saying "It looks like a really big shoo," the odd way he had of pronouncing the word "show."

Then, it was over -- four minutes, from start to finish.

EACH GUEST WAS ASSIGNED BY ME TO A specific talent coordinator, of whom there were four (myself included), and pre-interviewed in the booker's office, aside from a few movie stars from the Coast. They were usually seen in their hotel rooms.

There were only two exceptions: Buddy Hackett, who insisted on no preparation at all, which I always found somewhat disingenuous; surely, he must have done *some* thinking about what he was going to say, although he was brilliant enough not to have to. And Bob Hope, who used to call me the day before his appearance and rattle off a string of one-liners on various subjects, golf prominently among them.

After the pre-interviews, which generally lasted about twenty or thirty minutes, sometimes longer, the talent coordinator would give the matter serious thought, then dictate to his secretary what he, or she, wanted Carson to say. Very specific questions, in the rhythms of the host's speech, followed by their likely answers -- a unified summary of the guest's subject matter . . . leading, in an organic way, if possible, to the next questions and probable responses. And so on.

This provided Johnny with enough material to handle comfortably each guest's anticipated time on the air -- a total of around twelve to fifteen minutes (that's all), in two segments.

The secretary, in turn, typed it all up on a four-sheet, the first and second pages going to the producer, the third and fourth to the talent coordinator, who used them later to go over the earlier pre-interview with his guest.

The producer gave the first page, Johnny's copy, to the comedy writers, who wrote in suggested ad libs.

Later, he and Carson went over the whole thing, Johnny presumably writing in, or at least thinking of, more ad lib possibilities. Which is not to say he didn't make plenty of wildly funny remarks during the tapings off the top of his head. He did, and often. But no matter how it may have looked, ours was a very well-prepared, "spontaneous" show. As George Burns once said, "Sincerity is everything in this business. If you can fake that, you've got it made."

One of Johnny's ad libs *had* to have been unplanned. Shouting "Frontier *bris*!" when actor, Ed Ames, who played an American Indian on a television show, threw a tomahawk at a cardboard figure and caught it right in the crotch. It's anybody's guess as to how many people in the studio audience and the one at home knew what a *bris* is -- the traditional circumcision, among Jews, of their infant sons, within days of their birth.

On another occasion, we discovered a four-minute "hole" in an upcoming taping that no host, however resourceful, could be expected to cover on his own. What to do? *Where was Ed Sullivan, when you needed him?*

It wouldn't be right to invite another guest to come on for so short a time. Unless . . .

Georgie Jessel, as it happened, was to be on that night. I remembered that John Byner, a gifted comic, did a hilarious Jessel impersonation. (Bookers *live* for such moments.) We asked him, we were *compelled* to ask him, to deliver a   stand-up of only *three*-minutes -- usually, around eight minutes long; then, join the panel, but for only *one minute*, sitting next to Georgie, with both of them singing, as one voice in an echo chamber, Jessel's favorite song: "My Mother's Eyes".

It worked.

IMPERSONATIONS. OR ARE THEY "IMPRES-sions?" Professionals prefer the latter term, I believe, but they are virtually interchangeable. Almost anyone can do them, or think they can, and they have a remarkable shelf life.

For guys, there's always Cary Grant, chirping "Judy! Judy! Judy!" -- words he claimed never to have uttered in any of his movies. When we were in LA, I screwed up my courage to the sticking point and called him, inviting him on the show.

"I don't do television," he stated, sounding exactly as one might have expected, which came, in an odd way, as something of a surprise.

"You don't?" I said.

Scintillating.

"No," he said, and hung up.

Marlon Brando, of course. As Terry Malloy, in *On The Waterfront* ("I coulda been a contenduh. It was you, Charlie . . . "); then, scratching his jaw as *The Godfather*, a movie he made back in 1972!

And Jimmy Cagney, now and forever.

Adam Keefe, an inventive young comic, used to place Cagney in Yankee Stadium. He'd cup his hands to his mouth and exhale directly into the microphone, creating the sound of a roaring crowd . . .

cut it off with "You dirty rat!" . . . then return to the crowd, louder than before, now that Jimmy had put in an appearance.

Johnny himself did a superb Jack Benny, as well as the marvelous saloon comic, Joe E. Lewis. A legendary drinker and gambler, Lewis was once rushed to Manhattan General Hospital, so ill they gave him only a fifty-fifty chance to live. He insisted on being taken to Columbia Presbyterian, where, he claimed, "the odds were nine to five." It was there, he said, that they found "blood in my alcoholic stream." I once interviewed veteran comedy writer Eli Bass, who had come up with those lines, but he was such a dour character that I passed on him as a guest. A mistake.

Carson, unexpectedly, called me into his office, one time, and played a tape of his impressions of both Benny and Joe E., I nodding and smiling, he pleased, though trying not to show it. (Where he came from, you didn't make a fuss over your own accomplishments.) And I can make like Walter Brennan, which I did and do, at the drop of a hat. (Where *I* come from, you can't wait to.)

The fact is, impressions are a lot of fun and quite satisfying, maybe too much so. The sounds of W.C. Fields wannabes, drawling "My little chickadee . . . " are ever with us. (*vide*, Ed McMahon.) What it amounts to really is a kind of performance, by those of us who are not performers. And, hence, irresistible.

What really puzzles me is *how* it is done. I don't know anybody who recognizes his own voice, when it is played back to him.

"Is that what I sound like? I don't believe it!"

How then can someone be expected to "hear" another person's voice so well as to be able to reproduce it with such fidelity?

I *know* when I've got Walter Brennan right.

Once, on a whim, I tried to do Bill Cosby, while driving with a friend of mine, a black woman, who would know if I did it right -- an arguable presumption, the more I think about it.

"You got him!" she cried out.

I already knew it. Knew that I had caught not only the way Cosby sounded, but, without the benefit of a mirror, the way he *looked*, as well.

THE FIRST TIME BILL DID THE *TONIGHT SHOW*, Roy Silver, his personal manager, arranged for representatives from the top talent agencies to be there, to see first hand what all the shouting was about. Cosby reportedly did comedy unlike any person of color had done before him.

That night he did his lightly mocking "God" piece, in which the character he played -- was it Noah? -- talks to the Creator, in an amiable, if befuddled, fashion.

The studio audience loved it.

Roy told me how diligently the two of them had worked in honing Bill's persona, audio-taping all of his appearances while playing in various pit stops across the country. Dissecting his act with exquisite, unblinkered, care.

But the idea of being not so much a black comic, as a comic who was black, had to have originated with Cosby, to his everlasting credit.

It was much reflected in another of his standups, built around reminiscences of stickball games in the street, with the right fender of that parked car over there, first base, and the manhole cover straight ahead, second base, with other spots for third base and home. Describing kids at play: any kids, *all* kids. It's why, surely, the talented comedian has endured as long as he has -- at, or near the top, for over thirty years, by my reckoning.

Cos was also, from the beginning, very good as a sit-down guest, and in time, became one of the show's best ever. (Carson loved him.) He was not only a lot of fun, but nice to be with. Very much at ease with the audience, and with himself.

Except one time, when we were into a longish commercial break, Johnny having left the stage, presumably to go to the bathroom. (Where else *would* he have gone? Or maybe he got up merely to stretch his legs -- I don't know. It had never happened before, nor would it ever again.) Bill was still in the swivel chair, alone now with the guest that had preceded him, sitting on the couch.

Kaye Stevens was a pretty redhead, an actress-singer, with a companionable, if effusive, manner. Much taken with Cosby, she was given to poking him lightly on the arm and on the shoulder. Affectionately. No big deal.

Cosby was noticeably unresponsive towards her, however, never even turning his head in her direction, let alone participating in the kibitzing. He just stared straight ahead, looking very uncomfortable.

This was only his third appearance with us -- still early in the game -- at a time when a black man on TV, perceived as getting too chummy with a white woman, could be in a lot of trouble. Petula Clark's barely incidental physical contact with Harry Belafonte, at the end of their duet on her own show, caused a major brouhaha. Three Southern television stations had refused to carry it.

There was, of course, always the possibility that Bill's inattention to Miss Stevens was simply because he didn't care for the fuss she had been making over him. But if that were so, wouldn't he have been more likely to handle it lightly and politely?

No, it was his concern over what others might think, I believe, that caused him to turn away -- a reflex action, since we were off the air, with only the studio audience in attendance. He was probably trying to discourage her, by not *en*couraging her, from behaving in the same way, once we were back from commercial. And indeed she was properly subdued, even markedly so, thereafter.

It's hard to be certain about the matter. But even if it only approximates how I perceived it to have been, what an awful shame it was.

PERRY CROSS PRODUCED THE SHOW DURING most of Carson's first year. He was a delightful guy, funny, in a sly, off-handed way. Typically, as when, after talking up a favorite performer, say, whom everybody else proceeded to shoot down, he'd switch, effortlessly and seamlessly.

"That's what I said. The guy doesn't have it. Never did."

And if he got a call, in the middle of a production meeting, he'd grumble, "I thought I told you never to call me at the office . . . " We were taken in, unaware that it was his wife on the phone, and not someone he shouldn't be talking to. Catching on only when he shared a laugh with her, and asked about the kids.

There was steel in him, as well.

In a weak moment, at a taping one night, I behaved badly.

Perry had adjured us earlier about the perils of getting too involved with our guests -- i.e., caring too much about how well they did on the show. Some disappointments were inevitable, he pointed out, under the best of circumstances -- certainly with Johnny at the helm (though this was unstated), whose general inadequacy as an interviewer we were, by now, all too aware of.

On this particular occasion, Carson was way off, and my guest was in deep trouble -- who it was, I cannot recall.

I felt terrible about it.

I looked around and found a piece of cardboard, and wrote a single word on it, in large letters.

Moving a few paces away from Perry -- all the talent coordinators were clustered around the boom, within easy reach of the producer -- I positioned myself directly in Johnny's line of sight, holding the card to my chest. When he glanced at me, I pointed. He picked up the cue and ran with it, putting the interview more or less back on track.

Unfortunately, Cross saw the exchange of looks between us. And I saw that he saw us.

Perry said nothing, though his expression hardened. Me, I fled; scooted, was more like it, to a point somewhere between the set and the green room. And waited, feeling like a little boy, about to be punished. Sitting, figuratively speaking, with my thumb in my mouth.

It was, I realized -- how could I not? -- a damfool thing to have done, no matter that it worked out pretty well. As a subordinate, you just don't make that kind of move. It's bush.

During the next commercial break, a long one, Perry took care of business, briefly discussing with Johnny the next segment's guest, while moving the previous, ill-used guest over to the couch; and calling the booth, to touch base with the associate director, and through him, the director -- Carson's brother, Dick.

Finally, he headed my way. Unhurriedly. From my perspective, almost in slow motion. Soon enough, he was standing directly in front of me, his face still unreadable, though I thought he looked a little sad.

"On this show," he informed me, "there is only one producer. One."

With that, he pivoted and returned to the set.

Even at the time, I was struck by the way he had handled the situation. No big lecture, obviously; no threats, no self-serving displays of righteous indignation. Just making his point and letting it go at that. Telling it like it is -- a phrase already wildly popular, from the new show, *Laugh In*. If I was smart enough to get the message, fine. If not . . .

I got the message, although I never did get over those instances when a guest was made to look bad, for no damn reason.

On another day, I spoke to him in his office about the show, in general, still wondering, along with several of the others, whether Johnny was going to make it. How could he, a talk show host unable to *talk* to his guests?

Perry had no doubts.

"He'll get better. You'll see."

I'm not sure if Carson ever did. Not really, at least during the four-and-a-half years I worked on the show. But there's no question that he brought *something* to his interviews that often made them work.

What it was didn't occur to me -- if, in fact, I ever got it right -- until much later.

His opening monologues, however, were another story.

Posted on cue cards, propped up against the wall in front of him -- which is why he could be seen glancing down, then back up, after every comic observation -- they were funny and sharp, in what came to be the usual late-night TV mode, taking down every "dummy" who managed to stray within the host's ambit, which is to say, his firing range. The "jokes" played well with both his audiences -- the one in the studio, and the other one, at home.

More important, they liked *him*, from the start.

Johnny was easy to take. Not ethnic, or particularly show biz-y; not overwrought, like his predecessor, Jack Paar, or cerebral, like Steve Allen, who started it all.

But it was more than that.

His viewers quickly sensed, or assumed -- by his look, his demeanor -- that he was a regular guy, someone who came across very much as they would have, had they been as witty. A guy they could reasonably believe.

Thus, when he made a comment about them as perfunctory as, "Looks like a really good group . . . " they were disposed to assume he meant it literally. And when he took down the high and mighty, he was of course expressing their very own sentiments.

Johnny, the Giant Killer.

Even as they knew, as did he, how grand it would be to sniff the rarefied air of fame and fortune. If it was *them* he was going after.

In that, as with just about everything else, he and his audiences were soon remarkably complicit.

Ironically, in a very short time, *he* became one of the high and mighty, precisely because of their support and adulation. But that was okay. One of their own had made it. Good luck to him.

In his monologues, Johnny was arguably at his funniest when his jests and sallies *didn't* work.

When that happened, his audiences were emboldened to act up and act out, often groaning en masse, letting him know they were not happy. Laughing at themselves for behaving so outrageously.

But when Johnny came up with an especially cutting remark -- a zinger too far -- the "really good group" went so far as to jeer, stomp and whistle, as if they felt it was time to knock him off *his* pedestal.

Carson responded by looking mystified.

He turned to Ed, eyebrows raised: What brought this on? McMahon shrugged, as if he couldn't understand it either.

Up went the noise level a few more decibels.

Running out of patience, Johnny frowned and held up a hand. His audience quieted down immediately.

Presenting himself as the voice of reason, he pointed out that they had got into the studio for nothing, right?

"It didn't cost you anything, did it?"

There was a general murmur of assent, his fans sensing where he was going.

"Well," he said, nailing it down, "you get what you pay for!"

Screams.

What a guy!

Actually, it was when a joke really died -- when it *bombed!* -- that Carson showed his greatest resourcefulness, the studio audience making the kind of rumbling sounds which indicated that *this* time, they weren't kidding. Seriously.

In a progression in which each response encouraged the next, Johnny at first looked puzzled; then, the discontent appearing to intensify, bewildered; and finally, with a riot now apparently imminent, as if he was on the verge of -- was he kidding? -- flat-out panic!

Backing away uncertainly, his eyes darting about wildly, he said to Ed, out of the side of his mouth, but loud enough for all to hear: "Are they marching? Are they *advancing?*"

That stopped 'em, like spectators at a tennis match as play is about to resume.

Followed by a burst of laughter.

The clever fellow had outfoxed them again.

In such a manner did he demonstrate his remarkable capacity for making everything work for him, placing himself -- or perhaps it just worked out that way -- in a win-win situation. If what he said was funny, well and good; if it wasn't, well okay: so much the better.

Did he ever deliberately go too far with his zingers? I think so. But bomb intentionally? I doubt it. It's hard to believe a comic would, or could, do that. It goes too much against the grain. And too risky, in any case.

At the very least, though, Carson knew that were things to go badly for him, he could handle it. Beautifully.

FEW PEOPLE KNOW, OR KNOWING, HAVE LONG remembered that when Johnny started, a sizable number of stations took the show at 11:*15* PM, EST, the full network joining in at 11:30. It called for two separate openings, a hybrid arrangement nobody liked, which took NBC almost a year to rectify.

On October 1st, 1962, Ed McMahon stunned the audience at the earlier time by introducing as the show's host . . . Groucho Marx!. He did it again at 11:30 PM. But Groucho stayed on only long enough to turn the reins over to Johnny, with gracious good wishes. With Carson finally at the helm, the audience applauded enthusiastically.

The reason why it was done this way was so Johnny wouldn't have to do both openings on his first night hosting the show. With Groucho there, it was felt that some of the pressure would be taken off him, the old pro's presence helping to absorb the shock.

Carson *was* a little nervous, repeatedly making his funny little "a-huh! a-huh!" sound, deep down in his throat, sort of an abbreviated laugh, more like a cackle, captured so well by the impressionist, Rich Little, who actually did it better than Johnny.

Groucho, a beloved figure in the business, as well as among a whole lot of ordinary people, was on the show a few times, thereafter, as a guest. (He also guest-hosted the show once.) I assigned him to myself, my job essentially to shepherd him around and make him comfortable.

Marx was, I would guess, in his early sixties. Jessel's age. Not terribly old, really, but he *seemed* old. Off camera, he moved slowly and spoke softly, not carrying a big stick -- not at all disposed, as he was in his films, to leap in and make mincemeat out of other peoples' foolishness. (Perhaps he never was.) To the contrary, he was unfailingly kind and considerate. To everyone.

The problem?

Everybody *assumed* he was going to be funny, and started to laugh at what he said, even before he said it. Followed by an awkward moment, when they realized their anticipation had been misplaced. Feeling, perhaps, that they had done the legendary comedian a disservice.

If Groucho noticed it, he didn't seem to mind.

DOING THE SHOW PROVIDED ME WITH AN opportunity to meet some old screen favorites.

I pre-interviewed Jimmy Stewart in his hotel room. He asked if it was, uh, uh, all right to, uh, uh, play the accordion on the show. There was an undeniable, and unforced, twinkle in his eye.

I smiled and allowed that it would be.

Together with the comedienne Phyllis Diller on sax, and Johnny on drums, the trio came up with music not likely to make the world seem a better place.   But to watch Stewart squeeze, and unsqueeze, his instrument with such little-boy delight, as if he were giving a recital, was a treat all by itself.

Carson on drums, though . . .

It was not so much how well, or how badly, he played, but rather what a *chore* it seemed to be for him. No fun at all.

At the swivel chair, Jimmy recalled what happened when he was drafted in the early days of World War II. (Very early days. His was one of the first numbers called, if not the very first.) The trouble was, at six-foot-two, he weighed only 113 lbs. -- two pounds below the minimum.

"I had to, uh, uh, drink two thick milkshakes before they'd take me . . . "

"Really?" said Johnny, as if much impressed. "Two milkshakes, eh?"

"Uh-huh. That's right," Jimmy replied. He held up two fingers. "Two of 'em . . . "

Johnny (nodding): "Two. Thick. Gotcha."

Stewart looked as if he still felt he hadn't yet made his case.

" . . . and, uh, uh, a banana split!"

"A banana split!" Johnny echoed, no longer able to hold back his laughter. Clearly, he was delighted with his guest.

Jimmy, too, seemed pleased with the way things were going.

Two pros, spontaneously acting in concert. Enjoying themselves.

TWICE A YEAR WE DID THE SHOW OUT OF NBC Burbank, in California. Each time for two-week periods. I would go out ten days ahead of the others, to book all of the first week and most of the second. Later, I would leave Burbank early, while the rest of the crew stayed on, and repeat the process, getting everything ready for when the show would resume in New York.

At the office NBC supplied me, modest by their standards but commodious compared to the mini-cab I worked out of at 30 Rock, I started to sort out the many offers that had accumulated from Hollywood agents and managers, whose stars were, according to them, dying to do the show.

I then called Perry in New York and gave him an overview.

Every day thereafter, we spoke at two o'clock, five o'clock his time -- fifteen minutes before the second and final production meeting. We'd kick it around, and he'd make his choices -- as well as come up with some tentative possible bookings -- which I started acting upon the minute I hung up, bringing a little East Coast energy to the process.

There was a sizable number of letters waiting for me from nonprofessionals -- oddballs, for the most part; so-called kooks -- who were offering themselves to us.

A few stood out, one in particular, probably because of its subject matter. Extrasensory perception (ESP) has always interested me. How

37

else to account for those instances when you *know*, usually quite suddenly and often with a start, that someone is looking at you, even though he is nowhere in sight -- may actually be *behind* you -- and hasn't made a sound?

The letter was well-written. It struck a nice balance between pride and self-effacement.

Chan Thomas was a geologist, whom I assumed was Oriental -- Chan, as in Charlie. He claimed to have stumbled upon the secret of communicating in this unique fashion while doing whatever it is geologists do. I invited him in for an interview.

He turned out to be not Chinese at all: "Chan" was short for *Chandler*, dummy. A nice-looking fellow, he wore tortoise shell glasses and presented a pleasant, scholarly mien to the world. With him came a friend -- no surprise, there -- who nodded corroboratively at everything his main man said. Two, for the price of one.

Chan, in his soft-spoken way, was very impressive.

He told me that in his public appearances, he'd give a demonstration by picking out a member of the audience, usually a woman, and concentrate on communicating to her a single thought: *stand up*. After a while, to everyone's surprise, the designee raised her hand and tentatively rose to her feet.

I asked him if he could do something like that with me, here and now.

"I'll try," he said, "but please don't think about it. I'll slip a message to you during the pauses."

Well, then, I wanted to know, what *is* the secret of ESP?

Thomas shook his head.

"I'm afraid I can't tell you that."

Oh? Okay.

Are you able to use this technique in your everyday life? With your wife? Your children?

Yes, indeed. All the time, over vast distances.

"I'd be on the road and want her to do something for me -- you know, pick up some dry cleaning, or whatever -- and when I got home, there it would be. Hanging in my closet."

As the geologist laid it all out, he conveyed an air of quiet, almost unnerving, certitude.

"And the kids, too . . . "

Children evidently communicate extrasensorily on their own. As they grow older, and become more reliant on the spoken word, their ESP skills, understandably, begin to erode. These skills can be re-mastered, so to speak, which was now happening with his two boys.

We continued in this vein for several minutes. The more I heard, the more convinced I became that the spot would work, even if it turned out that Thomas was unable to deliver his own brand of mental telepathy during the show. It'd be fun, anyway, like when one of Johnny's monologue jokes didn't make it. And it was really interesting.

Suddenly, I had a thought -- out of nowhere. To rise up out of my chair!

"Chan," I said, "are you trying to make me stand up?"

He nodded, looking owlish.

"What'd I tell you?" his friend burst forth, his first words. Waiting for the right moment, I guess. He had probably been sending me the same damn message. No fair, two against one.

There was a possibility, admittedly, that the earlier reference to what he claimed had happened with the woman in the audience had stayed with me and was father to the thought. But as far as booking him on the show was concerned, it didn't matter. I told Mr. Thomas we'd be delighted to have him as a guest.

Later, when I spoke to Perry about it, he asked me if there was some way we could make the spot visual.

Yes.

Chan was going to bring with him a package, a small one, whose contents would be known only to him and me. During his appearance, he'd try to convey to Johnny what was inside it.

"Sounds good," Perry said.

Chan arrived for the taping with package in hand.

It was square, a box maybe 9" x 9", 6" deep. There was no way anyone could possibly guess what it held: a rare musical instrument, a German trumpet. Kind of squashed-looking; a miniature.

Thomas was the last scheduled guest.

When he made his entrance, he placed the box on the edge of Carson's desk.

"I'll try to get across to you what's inside it, as we go along, Johnny," he stated. "Try not to guess, though, 'cause that'll get in the way of the process. Just forget about it."

Johnny agreed, staring at the box.

"If I can."

Chan told his story, holding his audience nicely -- at the panel, and in the studio. He said that people communicate with ESP all the time, without even knowing it.

"You and Ed, for example. You two are clearly on each other's wave length . . . "

There was no disputing that. Nor was Carson disposed to. He was playing this one straight.

"I see something round," he said, indicating what might be inside the rectangular box.

Chan smiled, enigmatically.

Johnny asked if *he* could do it. ESP.

"You can try," Chan replied. He shrugged. "I wouldn't be surprised. Sure. Go ahead."

Johnny turned to Skitch Henderson, the leader of the *Tonight Show* band.

"Skitch, I'm sending you a message . . . "

Dick Carson cut to Henderson, who had an unlit cigar jutting from his mouth. He looked blank. At the boom, one of the technicians tapped me on the shoulder.

"Is it metallic? The thing?"

The little German trumpet inside the box was metallic.

By now, it was time to go to commercial, the last one of the show. When we'd come back, there would be only about fifty seconds to wrap it all up.

There was a buzz in the studio.

During the break, Ed McMahon got up from the couch and started chatting with Skitcher, who had crossed over from the bandstand. They were standing a few feet in front of the desk. Johnny was leaning in, apparently trying to catch the gist of their conversation.

"What!" he suddenly exclaimed, half-rising out of his chair. To Ed: "*What did you just say?*"

McMahon, not having a clue as to what Johnny was so excited about, explained.

"Oh, I was just telling Skitch that I had been sending him a message, too. To sit down and play 'Moonlight In Vermont.'" On earlier shows, he and

Carson had remarked several times how much the opening bars of that tune sounded like the opening bars of "Autumn In New York." They were a little nutsy on the subject.

Johnny couldn't believe it.

"But that's exactly the message *I* was sending him," he sputtered. "That's what *I* wanted him to do?"

When we came back from commercial, Carson tried to get across to the viewers what had evidently occurred. He had been attempting to send Skitch the thought -- play the opening bars of both tunes -- but Henderson didn't pick up on it, *Ed McMahon did!* Or vice-versa. It had originated with Ed and had insinuated itself into Johnny's unconscious.

The point was, *they* had communicated with each other, via ESP! That was the only logical inference one could draw!

Alas, we had no time to savor the moment. The show was just about over, and Johnny was compelled to say his good nights. After he did, everyone milled about, pumped up, not quite believing what had just apparently taken place.

I looked for Chan, who was still seated in the swivel chair. He looked very pleased with himself.

Time had run out, too, before he'd had a chance to reveal what was in the box.

About a year later, in New York, Thomas popped in for an unexpected visit. It was nice to see him. I asked if he was still fiddling with ESP. Indeed, he was -- more than ever. A guest was coming in for a pre-interview, so it had to be a brief encounter.

On his way out, Chan paused dramatically at the door, and turned back to me.

"By the way," he said, pointing heavenward. "It's true."

It took a beat for me to catch on.

"You mean -- are you saying? -- there *is* a God?"

"Oh, yes," he replied, in the manner of one who *knows*.

Then, smiling sweetly, he was gone.

SOMETIME IN MID-DECEMBER, ON A CHILLY winter's day, I found an unexpected package in the mail. It was postmarked Omaha, Nebraska, and contained six frozen steaks, packed in dry ice--brrr!-- no card, no nothin', to indicate who the sender might be. Since I didn't know anyone in Omaha, Nebraska, I assumed a mistake had been made, too late to rectify now that -- oops! -- the package had already been opened. I put the goodies in the freezer section of my refrigerator and counted my blessings.

The next day, I mentioned it to a couple of the guys at work. Each of them had received the same mysterious gift. Upon reflection, none of us had any doubt as to who our benefactor was. Johnny, of course. His secretary later confirmed it.

On the following Christmas, and the one after that, we all got six more frozen steaks, packed in dry ice -- with no identifying marks, as before.

Brrr!

BARBRA STREISAND MADE HER FIRST appearance on the show. Her first *meaningful* appearance.

She was going to sing, word had it, "Happy Days Are Here Again," which came as something of a surprise.

"Happy Days . . . " is an up-tempo tune, jaunty and exuberant -- not normally her kind of material. For years, it was (and still is) the theme song for the Democratic Party, going back to 1928, when Al Smith, then governor of New York, was a presidential candidate. So what was Miss Barbra doing, messing with it?

I had had an earlier connection with her, though I don't believe she ever knew it.

She had been a regular on the show I worked on before coming to the *Tonight Show* -- *PM*, with Mike Wallace -- appearing a couple of times a week and talking about herself -- a real, honest-to-God New Yorker, brash and brassy.

Self-consciously *un*selfconscious, she was. But in a way that made you smile, even as you scratched your head: Who was this unusual-looking person -- all of nineteen, at the time -- who spoke so comically about her threadbare wardrobe, the various outfits she put together. Using, she claimed, only secondhand clothes, bought dirt-cheap (for a song?) at secondhand clothing stores.

All this, before "Second Hand Rose," the number she was to sing later with such brio, in *Funny Girl*, had been revived.

Ah, but there you have it.

For when she sang, everything fell into place. Her voice was clean and pure -- thrilling, actually. And powerful.

Hell, she blew the goddam roof off!

And now? On the *Tonight Show*, she was going to sing "Happy Days Are Here Again?" It didn't compute.

What happened was, she came out and sang the song . . . as a *ballad*. A beautiful, haunting, poignant ballad -- which, as rendered by her, it was revealed to be.

The studio audience was overwhelmed. They couldn't stop applauding, rising to their feet spontaneously and giving her a standing ovation -- the only such ever.

Afterwards, I asked Marty Erlichmann, her personal manager, who it was that had come up with the idea of doing the song this way.

"She did," he told me, flatly. "She's a freeking genius."

And only twenty-one, twenty-two years old.

A word about how Miss Streisand's performance was staged by brother Dick, who sat her at a dressing table, in front of a three-way mirror, and shot her from every angle, including her profile. Yes, she had a prominent nose. So what?

I believe what he did signaled the beginning of a remarkable change in how Barbra came to be perceived by the public.

The sixties was a time of rampant narcissism. A lot of people -- or so it seemed; they drew so much attention to themselves -- made extravagant efforts at being eye-catching . . . the farther out, the better.

At the same time, they laid claim to a lofty spirituality, wherein only the inner person mattered. That was where real beauty resided.

But piety, once unleashed, has to go somewhere.

Its new target became, inevitably, *physical* beauty.

Whereas, heretofore, it was a good thing, even desirable, to be pretty or handsome, among these folks such attributes became automatically suspect. If you looked that good, you must be hiding something. "Dorian Grays" were everywhere, presumably, of both genders.

Conversely, if you were *not* physically attractive, it was presumed that you at least had a shot at being beautiful where it really counted. Conceivably, a Mother Teresa in waiting.

This kind of deep thinking led to a remarkable phenomenon.

Barbra's presumed inner beauty began to inform the perception, among many, of how she looked. All of a sudden, she was seen, she was described by many, as being -- well, beautiful. In an almost mystical, magical way, she went from putative ugly duckling to a personage out of Ancient Egypt, gamboling among the pharaohs. A regular Nefertiti.

Her profile appeared everywhere.

This perception served her well. It persists -- lingers? -- to this day, and is a testament to the power of an idea, even a foolish one, if enough influential people clamor for it and enough ordinary folk are stampeded into going along.

Or was it simply that styles were changing?

But style-makers pick up on, and then make their own contribution to, the zeitgeist, do they not?

They do.

LIZA MINELLI WAS ALSO A YOUNGSTER, AT THE time.

Only nineteen herself, she was making her Broadway debut, starring in a straight play -- a comedy, titled *Flora, The Red Menace.* It was directed by the legendary George Abbott, whom everyone called "Mr. Abbott," and who was still directing plays in his nineties. (He lived to be well past a hundred.) A remarkable gentleman.

Liza was coming in for a pre-interview.

I watched her arrive with her publicist, Pat Newcombe, and another young woman, who presumably was with Pat. The three ambled in my direction down the aisle between the desks occupied by the show's secretaries, with some of whom Pat dallied briefly -- an area infelicitously referred to as "the bullpen."

And Miss Minelli?

She looked bemused, I would say, patiently waiting out the slow procession trailing behind her.

When she spotted me, I thought I saw a slight hesitation. Her expression didn't change, but then it couldn't be expected to. She had never seen me before, didn't necessarily know it was me she was coming to see. And there had been no direct communication between us, everything having been arranged by her PR person.

As she drew closer, there was something about the tentative way she carried herself that suggested -- what was it? Vulnerability? I believe I may have, instinctively, opened my hands, palms up; may have raised them fractionally. Inclined my shoulders in her direction.

However it came to pass, she took a few purposeful steps towards me . . . and fell into my arms.

Just like that.

It wasn't a romantic embrace. More like that of a young woman much in need of comforting.

I held her; and she held me.

Of what followed, I have no recollection. Neither of the pre-interview, itself, or of what happened on the show. And I doubt if she'd remember any of it. It had probably been an instinctive act on her part. Whatever it was she may have needed, I happened to have been the one who was there to provide it.

Or maybe it was simply part of the new liberation: on meeting someone, a hug, instead of a handshake.

In a later appearance on the show, she performed a four-minute medley from *Cabaret*, memorable principally for its direct and unadorned presentation -- remarkably effective, as opposed to her "live" performances elsewhere. By that time, she had become the darling of the chi-chi Broadway crowd: LIZA! Everything she did was extravagantly over-produced and over-directed -- too smart, too charming, too precious.

Too much.

And, possibly, beyond the talents she brought to the fair.

I WAS READING *LIFE* MAGAZINE ONE DAY AND came upon a story about a young boxer, out of Louisville, Ky., named Cassius Marcellus Clay.

The photographs of Mr. Clay revealed a good-looking young Negro man -- the term "black" not yet in vogue, let alone "African-American" -- with the text delineating his already impressive record. It also detailed his penchant for two-line "poems" of his own invention, in which he picked the round he'd knock out his next opponent. Something like, "He'll be lucky to be alive, when he falls in five!" -- delivering, always, on or close to the appointed round.

I called his people in Louisville. They were very pleased to hear from us. Cassius was coming to New York in the near future for a fight at the famed Madison Square Garden. They were certain he could find time to squeeze us in. The match, against a very good heavyweight, Doug Jones, would be an important one for him, even pivotal -- a sizable stepping up in class. An event was in the brewing.

As word began to spread about Clay, it was clear that what really set him apart from all the other up-and-comers was that his manner, the way he comported himself, did not conform to what was generally expected of a young black man. He was neither shy, nor self-effacing, and didn't appear to know his "place." He even had the temerity to think highly of himself. In time, "I am the greatest!" became his battle cry.

I interviewed him in his hotel room.

Actually, he spent most of the time clowning around with his brother and a friend. Angelo Dundee, his savvy manager and trainer, was there, too. Five guys, crowded together in a very small room, with me fighting claustrophobia, or something very much like it -- an old problem of mine.

But I was impressed with Cassius, only twenty, twenty-one, who appeared to be very much at ease, though his handshake was spongy and his eyes rarely made direct contact.

Affable, but guarded.

On the night of the taping, I took him in to meet Johnny.

While waiting in Carson's office, with everyone buzzing around him, Clay spotted a blowup of a New Yorker cartoon, just above the table lamp. Two guys side by side, shackled to a wall maybe ten feet off the ground, with no possibility of escape. One is saying to the other, "Now, here's my plan . . . " Cassius burst into laughter, glancing every which way, wanting to share it. Looking very much like a man who had just come upon something he had never encountered before.

What was memorable about his appearance on the show was its climax, a "battle royal" between him and his challenger, Johnny Carson.

When we came out of commercial, Ed McMahon was sitting at Carson's desk. In stentorian tones, he introduced the pugilists -- first, Cassius; then, "Killer" Carson.

Out came Johnny, skinny in those days, wearing bright red trunks and boxing gloves, both way too big for him. Every time he raised his arms, in "triumph," his trunks started to fall down. Grabbing hold of them with outsized gloves wasn't easy, and the more he tried, the more frazzled he became.

Attention shifted to Clay. How was he going to react to all this folderol?

The young fighter glared into the camera, and waggled a finger.

"'Killer' Carson . . . will fall . . . in one!"

And smiled.

Piece o' cake.

A few nights later, Clay -- who later changed his name to Muhammad Ali -- defeated Jones, in a very close fight, which some people to this day think he lost.

AT HOME, FOR A VISIT.

Many of my friends and, surprisingly, some members of my family kept wanting to know what Johnny was really like, hoping for the inside story, the straight poop, the untold tale. But that's what I got from everybody.

I expected better.

There was also a lot of exclaiming over guests they "loved," in ways that suggested a substantial emotional investment, as if they were being evaluated by the choices they made. Which, to some extent, I suppose they were. By me, as well as by each other.

Some relatively offbeat appraisals were offered, the while carefully gauging my reaction. "How about X? He's pretty good, isn't he?" Relieved, when I agreed.

What floored me was the torrent of dissent I received.

"Why do you have that guy on the show? I hate him!" Or, "What about what's-her-name? I can't stand her."   Rat-a-tat-tat.   I struggled with it; occasionally, I exploded. Kidding.

"What? You don't like him? Well, that's it. He'll never do the show again!"

It got a few laughs, and fewer mumbled apologies, but it hardly changed anything. For the longest time, I couldn't figure out what they were so angry about. Until I realized comparable feelings in myself. And tales of opera stars being pelted with veggies, on an off night, go way back. Despite the fact that the players were surely doing the best they were capable of.

On the other hand, if someone presents himself to an audience, he is saying in effect that he will meet at least the minimum requirements *all* performers, of whatever stripe, are expected to live up to. A contract, admittedly implicit, has been entered into.

Consequently, failure to meet such expectations amounts to a breach of that contract. Audiences have a right, if not a duty, to register their objections.

Hurling invective, instead of cabbages, may be the only way open to them.

IT WAS TIME FOR PERRY CROSS TO LEAVE US. He was off to the Coast, to produce Jerry Lewis's much-anticipated new talk show for ABC. The network was desperate to achieve parity with NBC and CBS, and Jerry was hot! hot! hot! after his wildly successful two weeks hosting our show. Now, it was his turn.

Look out!

His contract with ABC gave him almost total autonomy -- a huge miscalculation. This was not

Lewis's territory, and genius is not automatically transferable. Jerry would have been a great talk show host, I believe. Not, however, if he was the one calling all the shots.

Sure enough, he came up with the ill-conceived notion of doing his talk show in prime time -- eight o'clock, Saturday nights . . . the kind of bold, audacious move Lewis just loved to make.

It had been tried before.

By Jack Paar, after he quit the *Tonight Show*, and Jackie Gleason (". . . and *away* we go!"), as a major segment on his half-hour, talk/variety show, which succeeded the hour-long show he had done that contained the memorable "Honeymooners" segment. And away he went, as did Paar -- both only lasting a few weeks.

How come?

Audience expectations, I would think. At least, then.

In prime time, television viewers expected to see a finished product -- clearly defined entertainment. Structured. Smoothly put together.

They counted on it.

Talk shows, by their very nature, are never that "professional" looking. They have rough edges. They are, or at least appeared to be, informal, anything-can-happen events, something to experience after the more traditional stuff. Dessert, really: an end-of-the-day bonus.

In the one, it's like going to the movies, or a concert, a play, without leaving the house. In the other, to a party -- and not a fancy, dress-up one, at that. In the company of real people, no matter once removed. A whole other thing.

Jerry had in mind to conflate the two, but he went about in a way that was guaranteed not to work.

What he did was place his show not in an auditorium, with around three hundred seats, as was the case with the *Tonight Show*, achieving some proportionality between the size of the audience and what they were watching.

Oh, no.

Lewis chose to do his show in an honest-to-God theater -- a splendiferous, imposing, cavernous place, with a vast auditorium and two, maybe three balconies, and a stage large enough for a touch football game. Barren, during the taping, except for Jerry and his guest, downstage, a small table between them, with the band off in the distance. Inevitably, they were dwarfed by their surroundings, particularly in the wide shots, of which there were a plethora. Deliberately, I think. To show off the sheer *size* of it all.

It was grandiosity run amok. Street kid from New York makes good, big time -- literally, as well as metaphorically.

And, unbelievably, with everyone, cameramen, ushers, floor managers . . . in tuxedos!

Go do an easy, informal, light-hearted talk show in such a setting. In formal attire.

Where was Perry Cross in all this?

Nobody in New York seemed to know.

Stories began to trickle back from the Coast. Of how Jerry didn't even *see* Cross for two weeks, after his producer had arrived in LA. And when they did get together, it was while Lewis was shooting baskets in his back yard, with most of his concentration on the hoop.

That sort of thing.

Obviously, Jerry had decided to produce his own show.

And Perry got lost in the shuffle.

The prime time experiment was a huge disaster, perhaps the biggest in the history of the medium.

I assume Jere drew some solace, if not satisfaction, from the dimensions of his failure. If you're not going to make it, you might as well get into the record books, while you're -- glub! glub! -- going under.

Many were gleeful. Perfectly understandable.

Oddly, I was not.

Well, maybe not so oddly.

There is method in why the Jerry Lewises of this world work so hard at ingratiating themselves with everybody. They know, instinctively, the dangerous game they are playing and that at some point they will likely need all the support -- all the *sympathy*, if it comes to that -- they can get.

ART STARK, WHO SUCCEEDED PERRY CROSS, had been Johnny's producer on the daytime show, *Who Do You Trust?*, which Carson had hosted for four years, prior to taking over the *Tonight Show*.

One could see the strong connection between them.

Art was not that much older than Johnny, but conveyed a certain gravitas, their relationship appearing to have father-son overtones. He could have been called a "father figure" to Johnny. And was.

Stark and his predecessor were pros. Each had been in the business a long time. Whereas Perry was quick and funny, Art was more the good listener -- a good audience -- very responsive to wit and humor.

Not a bad thing for a producer to be.

On the other hand, his manner was that of someone under a lot of control, too much so to make others entirely comfortable in his presence. And he did have a look about him that was, at times, forbidding.

Or was it that you never know what these quiet guys were thinking?

Maybe it was physiognomic.

A reasonably attractive man, Art had slit-like, reptilian eyes, a la Rex Harrison. They put one in mind of a lizard, waiting to pounce. Or maybe an iguana, basking in the sun.

For some reason I was not at all intimidated by him; rather, I had the feeling -- accurate enough, as it turned out -- that his gruff demeanor was a cover for the fairly sensitive person within. The iguana, despite its fierce countenance, is reputed to be a sweet, gentle creature.

We established an immediate rapport -- "Rappaport," some of us were saying, in those days -- that served us well during the time we did the show together.

Along the way, this tough cookie came to Johnny's rescue (from himself), in as neat a piece of diplomatic maneuvering as you could ever hope to see.

BOB HOPE DID THE SHOW MANY TIMES. MY "working" with him consisted of his calling me the day before and rattling off, as always, a string of one-liners. All I had to do was give Johnny some generic questions to ask, which he undoubtedly would have come up with by himself, my stating them explicitly merely making things a little easier for him. Like, "How's your golf game, Bob?" and, at the end of the interview, "Where're you off to now, Bob?" Both repeatedly found amusing Johnny's own, "So you've got *another* NBC Special coming up, eh, Bob?" That, of course, was why Hope was on the show. But I always found the question a little snide, even unkind, in the guise of harmless, good-natured teasing.

I, personally, got a special kick out of swapping jokes with the star while he waited to go on. It was a thoroughly egalitarian exchange, the laughter depending only on how funny the gag was, and how well told.

Not so with other comedians, at least of that era, from whom the best you could hope for was a flinty smile, and a "That's funny," stated as fact, without mirth. Making people laugh is what *they* did and nothing for civilians to try their hand at.

So there Bob would be, on the day of the show, sauntering off the elevator, fully made up and ready to go. Arriving early and by himself, needing no entourage. Breezily completing, over his shoulder, an impromptu conversation that had sprung up in the elevator, in the few seconds it took to get from the ground floor to the sixth.

I was always glad to see him, as were we all.

Mind you, Bob was not someone with whom you *communicated* a whole hell of a lot. He seemed to go from moment to moment, not dwelling unduly on any one over another, its particular nature of no special interest to him. Operating on instinct, basically. Motion, with little emotion, other than what was obviously called for, that everyone displayed. The game he was so enamored of, golf, served as a perfect metaphor for the way he appeared to live his life. Hit the ball, and then follow it, whichever of the myriad ways it might take him.

Case in point.

One night, when he made his entrance, the audience surprised us all by rising spontaneously and giving him a standing ovation -- looking as if they hadn't expected to, but there it was. Simply for being there, unlike the one Barbra Streisand had received, in response to her amazing performance.

It was, I think, an instance of accumulated appreciation for all the entertainment Hope had provided through the years. (A collective *homage*, if you will.) He was, and had been, an American staple for a long, long time.

Johnny, truly marveling at the ovation, said, "How about that, Bob?"

"Yeah, how 'bout that?" Hope replied.

He looked out at the audience, still standing and applauding.

"I wanna tell ya . . . "

The words were there, sort of, the sense of wonder and awe duly noted, but the comedian appeared to be curiously detached, almost diffident, about the whole thing. It's true that he had received many accolades throughout his career. But this one had to be different, if only for its spontaneity, for being so unexpected.

Hope stood up and took a small bow, his broad caricature of a grin in place. Then, he sat down, and turned to his host.

After a beat, everyone in the audience sat, as well.

The moment -- quite special, in its way -- was over, ending as abruptly as it had begun.

The most remarkable aspect of Bob's long career was his demonstrated capacity to play two discrete roles, diametrically opposed to one another, and doing both equally well.

In the *Road* pictures he made with Bing Crosby and Dorothy Lamour, he was the likeable shnook, a bumbler-fumbler with a wildly exaggerated sense of himself as a ladies' man -- the last guy in the movie to know he was *not* going to get the girl.

Whereas on television, he hosted his own specials and for many years the Academy Awards, kicking off each with a fast and furious, if not always hip, commentary on the passing scene. Looking good, a winner. At the top of his game.

Same guy, on two totally disparate tracks.

No one else has ever even tried to do it.

When Carson and I finally parted company, Bob conveyed to me, via his New York PR guy, how sorry he was to see me go. "He's the only one with any brains on that show," I was told he said. Not true, but nice to hear, I cannot tell a lie.

And after all this time, I still find myself using two of his favorite lines: "I'll be there with bells on. I'll look silly, but I'll wear 'em anyway . . . " And, "You can't keep a good man down. And you can't keep me down, either."

How 'bout that?

JOHNNY, TO HIS CREDIT, WAS NOT AT ALL difficult when it came to booking guests. There were only a few with whom he was so unhappy that he actually balked at their doing the show.

One, for a while, was Tony Randall.

He was a great guest, a self-starter, not at all dependent upon Carson's interviewing skills. Just ask the first question and watch him go.

Tony had a unique point of view on many things and was charmingly self-absorbed. You never knew where his nimble mind would take him. He also had a fey quality, which might have discomfited Johnny, but didn't. Carson enjoyed Randall's company.

On one show, however, Johnny evidently felt that Tony had gone too far, though while it was happening what the actor did appeared to be relatively innocuous.

During Randall's interview/monologues, it was not uncommon for him to interrupt himself and go off on a tangent.

In this instance, without establishing a predicate that could have given Johnny some warning, he suddenly leaned forward and began to examine Carson's head. From all sides, even asking his host to turn this way and that.

"Hmm," he said. "Who cuts your hair?"

Johnny didn't get it. Who *asks* such a question?

"No, I mean it," Randall said. "He's good, very good. An excellent haircut. Every hair in place . . . "

A few members of the studio audience tittered.

Carson didn't like the whole business.

It looked like he thought that in some obscure way, and for some damned reason, Tony was trying to make him look ridiculous. For an instant, Johnny flared up, so briefly it hardly registered, though we who knew him well could see how agitated he had become.

Randall, innocent of any malign intent -- he was just *talking*, for heaven sake! -- went back to whatever he had been going on about, before his brief excursion into personal grooming.

"Let's see, where was I?" Suddenly remembering, with a loud chuckle: "Oh, yes!"

Johnny completed the interview, and that appeared to be that. It wasn't.

After the show, in his office, he exploded.

"Randall's out! I never want him on the show again!"

I don't know how Stark reacted to Carson's uncharacteristic outburst, whether he challenged him on it, or not, but when he mentioned it to me, you could see that he found the blanket injunction against Tony absurd.

In any event, Randall didn't appear on the show for what turned out to be a whole year.

One day, we were hunting for a male guest Johnny could have some fun with. No one was around. I went through my lists and spotted Tony's name, struck by how he had pretty much disappeared from our consciousness. I brought it to Art's attention.

The producer buzzed the star.

"Tony?" Johnny said, over the speaker phone. "Sure! He'd be fine."

Apparently, the host had forgotten about his earlier grievance. His tone did convey a measure of wonder. Now that you mention it, where *had* Randall been all this time?

What we didn't know, of course, was *when* Johnny had forgotten about it. Maybe we could have brought the exiled actor back a lot sooner.

When Tony next did the show, he was as lively as ever, once again a valued guest.

ANOTHER GUEST JOHNNY HAD A PROBLEM with -- a real one -- was Tommy Smothers.

The Smothers Brothers, with Dick on bass and Tommy on guitar, were folk singers and good ones, but their act revolved principally around the comedy which was generated in the pauses between numbers by Tommy's mindless but amusing chatter.

Playing a dumb bunny who didn't know it, he was funny in a vaguely disturbing way, the audience laughing as much at him as with him. No matter what, he stayed the course, getting more and more mired in his own meanderings. His brother Dick "helped" by egging him on, demanding endless clarifications.

After a while, the audience, though still enjoying the brothers' to-and-fro, began to worry about the gabby one, who by now appeared to be in considerable distress.

Tommy was very good at that.

For several reasons -- probably that one, as well as the general air of contrivance that characterized the whole act -- I found his performance, his very persona, irritating.

Then again, and to be fair, the tension he and Dick created was intentional, stoked deliberately, up to and beyond the breaking point. When the audience began to show signs of becoming very restive, even as they continued to be amused -- which is to say, at exactly the right moment -- the brothers broke it off and reprised the song they had been singing, before Tommy had gone into his dance. Closing out their appearance on a rousing musical note, the traditional big finish, which more or less succeeded in relieving the tension they, themselves, had created.

Blew it away, you might say.

In so doing, however, Tommy's skill at the guitar, the competence with which he delivered the lyrics, his generally knowing air as a performer, gave the lie to his pervasive dimness only moments before. Or at least raised doubts about it -- undermining the "sincerity" with which he had presented himself.

It was a chancy business.

And it galled Johnny. Both it's reckless nature . . . and the fact that Tommy seemed to be getting away with it.

More important, Carson believed strongly that a performer -- particularly a stand-up comic, who of course bore all of the act's responsibility -- had an obligation to play it straight with his audience. Mess with their minds, yes, which was a given. But only so long as you let them in on it, in the various ways available to comedians. Bob Hope's "But, seriously . . ." after making an outrageous remark, comes to mind.

It was a complicated idea, but as Carson saw it, Tommy did his "ninny" bit too well, making it *un*clear as to whether or not he was only kidding. The brothers, by so egregiously manipulating the audience, were disregarding the rules of the game.

It didn't help that, on a particular occasion, Tommy got one of the biggest laughs in the history of the show.

After the brothers completed their act, Johnny invited them to join the panel. Seated at the far end of the couch, Tommy acknowledged the kind words everyone was saying to them, particularly Bette Davis, who had never left the swivel chair, at her insistence, the guests that followed sitting on the couch to her right -- the way it had been for Ed Sullivan, with Earl Wilson and Joey Adams. To Miss Davis, now some distance away, Tommy let everyone know what a great honor it was for him and Dick to be on the same show with her. Evidently still in character, his speech quickly evolved into a long, meandering paean to the famous actress and her distinguished career.

The audience couldn't quite figure what to make of it, laughing uncertainly at first and for a while thereafter, until they evidently concluded that Tommy *was* being serious, that he really meant what he was saying.

They listened, hushed.

As did the panel, particularly Miss Davis.

The inexhaustible Smothers brother finally wrapped it up.

"So, let me say again, Bette -- if I may call you Bette . . . " -- she nodded -- "what an honor it is . . . to be with you. Here. On this show."

The superstar looked genuinely touched. She bobbed her head and thanked him for *his* more-than-kind words.

"You're welcome," Tommy murmured, apparently moved as well. He took a moment to collect himself.

Then, he said, without ceremony:

"*Do you fool around?*"

Everyone gasped and immediately looked over at Miss Davis, whose popping eyes popped wider. Recovering quickly, she threw her head back and laughed her hard, barking laugh. And kept on laughing.

As did everyone else.

While Tommy looked oblivious to the stir he had created. A ninny, to the end.

(For one wild moment, I wondered if it was possible that he talked this way *all* the time.)

Johnny laughed, too -- he had to -- but his heart wasn't in it. Art Stark smiled grudgingly, not particularly amused. He caught Johnny's eye and nodded at the camera. Carson's "We'll be right back" ended the segment.

Not a moment too soon.

THE DIFFICULTIES JOHNNY HAD WITH BUDDY Hackett ran deeper, and were more visceral.

What it boiled down to was that Hackett was funny in a way Carson never could be, stemming not only from the differences in their background and temperament, but even more, I think, from how uncommonly sure of himself Buddy was, or appeared to be -- to the point of arrogance, not to say craziness, altogether.

This was markedly different from, and dwarfed, Johnny's sense of *him*self. Buddy's self-confidence was supreme; a mere mortal, Johnny's was something less than that.

Hackett being able to make an appearance allegedly without any preparation -- the kind of thing beyond Carson's power to even consider, let alone emulate -- also made him uneasy during the show, never quite certain where Buddy was headed.

Take what happened on a New Year's Eve show we did.

It came on a Thursday that year. Somebody realized that if the show we taped at the usual time could be aired the *next* night, Friday, we could get a four-day weekend out of it, and have a little end-of-the-year fun, ourselves . . . *if* NBC okayed our doing the New Year's Eve show "live."

They loved the idea.

So did we, although starting at around 10:30 in the morning and ending at one o'clock the following morning, January 1st, would make for a very long day.

After taping the earlier show, which ended at eight PM, we dallied in various ways for nearly three hours, returning to the studio at around quarter of eleven, no later than 11PM, when the guests would be arriving for the "live" show's start at eleven-thirty. Because of the festive occasion, Johnny was going to go straight from his monologue to bringing out his guests. And who better to usher in the New Year with than Jayne Mansfield and Buddy Hackett? Nobody. Together, they would be a hoot.

Party time!!!

Hats and horns!!!

It was not to be.

Since we weren't being taped, there would be no way to control what went out over the air. Buddy, it was felt, could not be trusted to restrain himself in the company of the ample sex symbol.

The two would *not* be on at the same time.

I liked Jayney a lot, genuinely, and not only because her breasts could make a grown man cry (and a child like me weep inconsolably.) She was a very sweet gal, and a lot smarter than generally given credit for, the squeaky, little-girl voice she used publicly pure affectation. That it didn't exactly go with her formidable presence was saved by her conveying a sense of the comic about it. Absent that, I too might well have found the pose a bit much.

Once, arriving for a pre-interview, she caught sight of herself (in a remarkable coincidence) on my telly, as a celebrity guest on a game show.

"Look at her!" she said disdainfully, in a voice that didn't squeak. "Oh, Lord!" But then, she laughed at one of her successful ripostes, laced with the inevitable sexual innuendo -- which the audience certainly seemed to enjoy -- her natural good humor quickly restored.

Ours was a friendship, if it could be called that, of the sort peculiar to people in show business, in that it thrived on being discontinuous. Seeing someone infrequently tends to keep the connection evergreen, leaving one generally disposed to draw upon pleasant associations, remembrances of only the good times. That's probably why people in the industry greet each other so effusively, with air kisses and all. On a catch-as-catch-can, occasional basis, Darling, it *is* good to see you!

On this day -- my second pre-interview, as was the case with all the talent coordinators, the one for the taped show done earlier -- Jayne told me, with irrepressible girlish enthusiasm, that she had become "Vice President of a meat company," her task -- what a shock! -- to "you know, inspect the meat." She made this pronouncement ostensibly innocent of its implications and its likely effect on the audience. Proud, she was, of her new title. You could tell by the swelling of her chest.

Mama mia!

This affirmed the wisdom of keeping Jayne and Buddy apart.

Or did it?

I honestly don't think Hackett would have got involved.

His strength did not lie in reacting to and commenting on others -- as did Johnny's. If he was going to say something "bad," it would originate with him, from the depths of his own comedic sensibility.

Buddy worked alone.

On the other hand, coupling Jayney with our third guest, Rudy Vallee, could be kind of fun, insofar as the audience ever saw a guest *together* with the one that preceded him, now seated to his immediate right. That would depend on Dick Carson taking the two-shot of Vallee and Mansfield, side by side, whenever it made some kind of sense to do so. Which he did.

Rudy had been one of the pioneers of radio, the first "crooner" of his time, using a megaphone *before* radio, to amplify his pleasant singing voice. Latterly, he played the simp in movies as if born to the role. Vallee was in fact a true eccentric. It was said of him that he actually had a coin-operated coke machine in his rumpus room.

He turned out to be an easygoing and likable guest, somewhat on the order of Tony Randall, though not nearly as bright, or as interesting. Coming on after Jayne, the two made a beguiling study in contrasts. Beauty and the Doofus, you might say.

At the end of Rudy's segment, they both said their goodbyes, wishing everybody a "HAPPY NEW YEAR!" and left, to "heavy mitting," Variety's amusing term for beacoup applause. Their departure was taken in stride; people come and go at a party all the time.

Now, it was Buddy's turn.

The network's case of the jitters about him had by this time extended to when he was going to be on alone, even without Jayne Mansfield around.

Sensing the situation, Hackett rose to the occasion, displaying his true storyteller's gift for making whatever tale he was telling diverting and alive. His text, often complex and rich in texture, was so well constructed as to be entirely clear and compelling.

He was, as well, gracious.

While making Stanley Kramer's *It's A Mad, Mad, Mad, Mad, Mad World*, he had, he said, spent some time with fellow actor Eddie "Rochester" Anderson, Jack Benny's long-time "chauffeur," going all the way back to Benny's radio program, and after that, his television show.

"Rochester," no longer young, had a serious hearing disability, which he tried to disguise by saying "Ba-zay!" to any comment made in his direction, any question asked.

"Ba-zay!"

It soon became the cast's buzzword, used in every conceivable situation.

"Ba-zay!"

There was no way, unfortunately, of ascertaining how the veteran comic actor felt about it, or indeed if he was even aware of what was happening. Somehow, Buddy managed to make the story both funny and touching, lightly laughing in his reminiscences, while conveying how sad it was that it had come to this for the aging performer.

The *Tonight Show's* studio audience was totally caught up in Hackett's recitation. And the way he comported himself reinforced my conviction that he would not have gone astray, had he been coupled, in a manner of speaking, with Miss Mansfield.

Oh, he might have thought about it, and feinted in that direction -- making a mildly salacious aside, or two, to show that he was not unaware of Jayne's presence -- but probably no more than that. If only because he knew that everybody at NBC expected it of him.

After the show, I congratulated him, and expressed my admiration.

"You wanna know how come?" Hackett asked. He sounded peevish, most likely a post-partum letdown, and still pissed over being in this position, in the first place. "Because I'm the best, that's why." That made him the third comic to have informed me they were the best, or was it the fourth? But on this night, indisputably, he was.

I hurried to my office on the seventh floor, grabbed my overcoat, putting it on as I scrambled back to the sixth floor, on my way to Johnny's office, going through studio 6B, now empty and looking eerily moribund. Art and I still had a New Year's Eve party to go to.

There, I encountered an unhappy-looking Joanne, Johnny's wife, sitting in her fur coat on the chair next

70

to the star's desk . . . a disgruntled-looking Art Stark, in *his* overcoat, standing a few feet away . . . and Johnny, clearly nettled, and saying, probably not for the first time, "Buddy's funny, Art. I know that. But . . . "

It was now twenty past one A.M., New Year's Day.

I got the sense, later confirmed, that this never wholly explicit refrain had been going on since the end of the show.

But for what reason?

Buddy had *not* misbehaved this night. His only crime was that he had been brilliant.

Reason enough.

Johnny's grumbling went on for another ten, fifteen minutes, an absurd display of pique which, as he well knew, was holding up two stalwart (if overtired) partygoers from getting it on. Finally, at about a quarter to two, Johnny said, for the last time, "Buddy's funny, Art, but . . . " and we got the hell out of there.

To be sure, Carson's distemper was, in a way, understandable, even apart from his own personal involvement. Prolonged exposure to the Buddy Hacketts of this world leaves everyone feeling depleted. These guys suck the air out of the room, their engines never off, even when they're not saying anything.

As we approached the exit doors of 30 Rock, there were, remarkably, still a few autograph seekers waiting to be thrilled -- at 2AM, of a cold winter's night. Carson scribbled his name a couple of times, and, as we crossed the street to his waiting limo, the use of which he had earlier graciously offered to Art, came up with a few, funny putdowns of "idiot" fans.

You could see that he was feeling better.

Joanne, Johnny and Stark sat in the back, with me in the passenger seat, next to the driver.

71

"Going to a party, eh, Art?" Johnny asked.

Stark grunted.

A few minutes later, we dropped the star and his wife off at their apartment, and said good night, wishing each other a Happy New Year. I got in the back seat, with Art, and gave directions to the driver.

"You know," I speculated, "I have the feeling that had I asked Johnny and Joanne to join us, they would have come along. I think so. Yes. New Year's Eve, and all by themselves, with no place to go."

Stark stared straight ahead.

"Fuck 'em," he said.

CARL REINER, WRITER, DIRECTOR, BRILLIANT straight man to Mel Brooks, and father of Rob, came up with a remarkably inventive conceit on one of our shows.

On overhearing that there would be only two minutes of the show remaining after we came back from commercial, he asked if we could try something he always thought might work in just such a situation.

"We three will just look into the camera, for whatever time remains. That's all. Not saying a word." Phyllis Newman was the other guest.

And that's what happened.

For the next minute and forty seconds -- a long time, on television, particularly without any sound, except for what might be forthcoming from the studio audience -- Dick Carson went from Camera #1, to Camera #2, to Camera #3, back and forth, catching Carl, Phyllis, and Johnny staring right back at 'em.

The laughter kicked in immediately, but it was small and sporadic. Then, it began to build on itself, finally cascading, until, by the time the experiment ran out -- the performers fulfilling their tasks perfectly, just looking into the camera, *without any change of expression* -- the whole place was breaking up.

Falling apart!

So was I.

Go figure.

THE SUBJECT WAS ROSES, A PLAY BY FRANK Gilroy, opened on Broadway to critical acclaim.

It was about a father and son -- the young man newly home from the war -- attempting to resolve old conflicts, under markedly changed circumstances. A familiar theme, but rendered beautifully, simple and direct.

The father was played by the fine character actor, Jack Albertson, later "The Man," in the successful TV sitcom, *Chico And The Man*. Irene Dailey, Dan Dailey's sister, was the mother; and the young Martin Sheen played the troubled son. The five New York papers netted one good review; a second, very good; and the other three, damn good. There was every reason to believe that the play could look forward to a comfortable run.

Yet, the first week's grosses were only $2,000. And the second week's, $2,200.

To put that in context, *Roses* was playing at a small, intimate theater, whose top weekly gross -- what its revenues would come to if every seat in the house was sold out, for all eight performances -- was $40,000.

With a cast of only three, and none of them stars, commanding big salaries, its "nut," the amount it had to take in to cover its weekly costs -- to break even -- was around $16,000. A one-set play, it had been capitalized at the relatively small sum of around $80,000. Meaning that, if the play was a smash, it could pay back its original investment in only four or five weeks!

But with each of its first two weeks' box office take a combined $14,000 *under* the break-even point, disaster loomed.

Something had to be done.

I discussed it with Art, who agreed.

We knew that Jack Albertson was a former vaudevillian. Maybe he and Johnny could do vaudeville shtick, which Carson loved, according to Stark -- particularly "crossovers."

That's where two performers enter from opposite ends of the stage, meet in the middle, and have an exchange on the order of the venerable "Why did the chicken cross the road?" "I don't know. Why *did* the chicken cross the road?" Answer: "To get to the other side!" The punch line was always punctuated by a rim shot on the drums -- ka-boom-boom! -- the straight man looking out at the audience and shouting "*What the hey!*", a sanitized version of "What the hell!" Vaudeville was considered proper adult entertainment -- often bawdy, even spicy, but never vulgar.

Albertson proved to be a winning guest, promoting his play, as to be expected, but entertaining the audience as well with tales of his early days in vaudeville. And the updated, smart-ass crossovers that the show's writers came up with, at which Johnny was remarkably adept, were a gas.

Because it went so well, we were justified in booking Jack for two more appearances, three in all, over just a five-week period! A record, of sorts. The

6:30PM taping was early enough for Broadway folk to appear on the show, always as Johnny's first guest, after which they were whisked to the theater in time for their opening curtain.

As a result of our efforts, there was an immediate and considerable jump in *Roses'* box office. And while the play never took in much more than its weekly nut, and didn't ever earn a profit, it had a respectable run, providing employment for its deserving cast and a solid showcase for the playwright.

All in all, a very gratifying experience.

Subsequently, I saw Jack and his wife, at a screening. He nodded in my direction, and mouthed "Thank you." I smiled and nodded back.

It was a nice moment, and more than enough for me. Although, a small plaque in my honor, nothing fancy, would have been nice. "Dedicated to S.K., without whose tireless efforts --"

Rim shot: ka-boom-boom!

"What the hey!"

THERE WAS THE TIME I WAS CHATTING WITH Joe Williams, the great jazz singer, he and I the only ones in the Green Room. We could hear, in brilliant, staccato bursts, the wonderful *Tonight Show* band warming up. Music to my ears.

The singer, Jane Morgan, joined us.

She was a fine figure of a woman, and a helluva dame, whom you could do worse than cast as a saucy barmaid in a Restoration Comedy. The one whom all the rascals covet, but for whom they have too much respect to -- you know: *go too far.*

A lusty wench.

While we chatted, I kept listening to the band.

When they began to play a tune straight through, I turned away from Joe and Jane, all my attention now on the great sounds which were engulfing me. The run-through over, I turned back and murmured, "How sweet it is!" -- referring, of course, to the way the band had cooked.

At that precise moment, Jane, knees dipped, was leaning into the low mirror behind the couch, to get a better look at herself. Revealing much.

She smiled at me, eyes atwinkling, evidently assuming, understandably, that my remark was meant for her -- as real and spontaneous a compliment as she had ever received.

What was I to do -- explain that it was the music I was celebrating? Particularly when "How sweet it is!" could just as easily have applied to her magnificent bosom?

I smiled back, coloring, fighting an urge to explain. Joe Williams got the picture. His rumbling, full-throated laughter filled the room.

BERNARD. HAIRDRESSER TO THE STARS. Reminiscent of Joan Rivers's divine inspiration, "Mr. Phyllis," whose parents always wanted a girl, ". . . and they got one."

Inevitably, he arrived late and was seen moving in haste, taking quick, mincing steps in the direction of a particular dressing room, wherein an anxious guest waited to be transformed.

Afterwards, in the heightened atmosphere of just-before-show time, with people in and out of makeup and agents and friends milling around in the corridor, he'd wrap his arms around me, from behind.

"Bernie," I'd say, wearily, "I've told you, I'm not interested. It's not my game . . . "

"Don't knock it, 'til you've tried it," he insisted, rolling his eyes.

I disengaged his grip from around my waist, laughing. I had heard it before. From him.

He laughed too.

Bernard (not his real name), who did much to dispel whatever discomfort I may have felt in the company of the flamboyant homosexual.

THEN THERE WAS HELEN GURLEY BROWN.

She had written a book called *Sex And The Single Girl*, a manual for single women -- or any woman, from what I could see -- on how to manipulate men. It offended me right down to my toenails.

Why then did I assign her to myself? That very anger, I suppose. It was a mistake, and I apologize for it.

(Better late than never? Uh-uh.)

Anyway, the pre-interview went as badly as one might have expected.

She was pumped up, gushing, the book a best-seller, and all. Very much the belle of the ball. Either I was masking my antipathy better than I thought I had been; or she wasn't picking up on it, being so full of herself; or she was remarkably forbearing.

Perversely, her sailing along, blithely ticking off one trick after another by which the wily female could trap the unsuspecting male, irritated me all the more.

Finally, I challenged her.

She fought back, stating she didn't see anything wrong with what she was doing. Not at all! She was providing a *service*, for heaven's sake!

"I don't like it, either," she insisted, meaning the manipulating. "But we all do it. I'm just showing women how to go about it *successfully*!"

I asked her where the sex was in the book. Her attitude towards the single girls she was advising was that of a fussy, super-chaste chaperone at a beauty contest -- all rules and winning stratagems -- the young ladies in her charge treated as stick figures. Bloodless.

Oh, but that's not what she was writing about, she protested. No, no, no. That part of the equation, the sexual, didn't particularly interest her at all.

"Besides," she added, taking insufficient care, "I don't understand what all the excitement's about. It's hot and it's sweaty, and the whole thing is over in six or seven minutes . . . "

Oh, my!

We both stopped talking -- she, coloring; me, embarrassed for her.

I climbed off my high horse, and we quickly wrapped it up in a conciliatory fashion, making the best of a bad situation.

The whole thing never should have happened.

ANOTHER TRIP TO THE COAST.

This one was planned to coincide with NBC's promoting its new fall lineup, in those days a very big deal, the networks dominating prime time, no cable to compete with. Big bucks were involved in how well the season kicked off.

Among the stars available to us was the distinguished character actor, Lee J. Cobb, co-starring in a new Western, one of several oaters still dominating the schedule. At their peak, there were as many as thirteen on the air, each and every week.

From the moment we met, Mr. Cobb -- sans toupee and, in manner, rather shy and self-effacing -- expressed the concern, the conviction, that he was going to be a lousy (his word) guest. He really didn't have anything to talk about, he told me, and was ill-suited, in any case, to the task.

"I'm not a schmoozer," he said.

Uh-huh.

Every talent coordinator had heard that kind of disparaging self-assessment before. And its obverse, the guest who sees himself as such a mine of surefire material that he feels a pre-interview is hardly necessary. "Johnny can ask me anything," he says, genuinely trying to be helpful. "Anything at all."

What he doesn't know is that Carson, on his own, rarely had anything in mind *to* ask.

"I understand," you tell him, "but let's have a little chat, anyway, okay? How do you like your coffee?"

In most cases, I believed -- a little smugly, perhaps -- that our pre-interviewing skills were sufficient to get past both obstacles. Dig down deep enough, in a non-threatening manner, and something worth sharing with others was bound to emerge.

Unfortunately, aside from talking about his new show -- thin gruel, at best -- and the fact that the actor and his wife were "considering" a nationwide tour of Shakespeare -- not exactly *Tonight Show* fare, on a good day -- Cobb was right. Despite my strenuous efforts, and his, nothing else showed up on the radar screen.

Lee, a very nice man, felt terrible about it.

"You know," he observed, "I hardly ever see the show these days. We shoot so early in the morning that I can't stay up that late anymore. All I get to see now is" -- he smiled -- "Johnny's 'It was so cold . . . ' jokes."

Bingo!

During his monologues, for those of you just tuning in, Carson would sometimes talk about the weather, when it was either very cold or very hot, depending upon the season.

"It was so cold that . . . " he'd say, finishing it off with something outrageous or silly (or both), like " . . . they had to put a fur-lined jock strap over the fig leaf on the statue outside Rockefeller Center." Better than that, usually, but that's the idea.

On one occasion, after Johnny had said, "It was so cold that . . . " and paused, Ed McMahon, whether by accident or design, asked: "How cold was it?"

Carson blinked and looked around, as if he knew he had heard something, but wasn't quite sure what it was. His expression also reflected disbelief: Did somebody actually *interrupt the monologue?*

"Pardon?" he said.

Ed was now compelled to repeat the question, which he did with new emphasis: "*How . . . cold . . . was . . . it?*"

Johnny waited, and waited some more, before answering -- an old Jack Benny trick. Then, he delivered the punch line.

Just like that, a ritual exchange was born, with countless variations and permutations to follow, under-girded by Carson's superb comic takes. It reached a point where the setup was as much anticipated as the jokes themselves.

That's what Cobb had been referring to.

I figured, why not have *him* do some "It was so cold . . . " jokes? It could be great fun! And we had nothing else.

Lee was less than enthusiastic about the idea, never expecting to play the comic on the *Tonight Show*. It was not, to be sure, his natural metier.

Ah, but that's where the fun would be.

What I had in mind was that at a certain point in the interview, the actor would state, matter-of-factly, "You know, Johnny, I was in New York recently, myself. And I was struck by how cold it was -- I mean, for this time of the year."

Carson (after a beat): "Oh? How cold was it, Lee?" Playing Ed McMahon, a nice touch.

Lee would then whip out the half-dozen cards on which his punch lines would be written, and go through them, one by one, giving each full measure -- waiting for the laughs, and allowing Johnny time to exploit the situation.

On the night of the show, however, as he was going over the funny lines the writers had supplied him, the comedian, Joey Bishop, with whom Cobb was sharing a double dressing room, wandered over. After observing his roommate's obvious discomfort for all of thirty seconds, Bishop shook his head, and intoned:

"It's not for you, Lee."

Cobb leaped up.

"See? What'd I tell you? Joey's right! And he's a *professional* comedian!"

"Okay," I conceded, the game clearly over. "The weather jokes are out. Joey *is* right . . . " I gathered up the cards. "Don't worry, Lee. Everything'll work out fine." (Ooh, such a liar!)

I sought out Stark and told him about it.

"Now, we've really got nothing," I wailed.

Art shrugged, signifying that it was too late to do anything about it now, so -- *what the hey!*

The show started.

Joey was the first guest.

The banter between him and Johnny was quick-witted enough, but the tone was all wrong. They were too competitive with one another, and it showed.

Next came Zsa-Zsa Gabor.

She was . . . Zsa-Zsa.

Which was also okay, although she claimed the guys were picking on her. That's because they were.

Now, it was Lee's turn.

As he made his entrance, there was, to my surprise, a gleam in his eye. All of them -- Johnny, Joey, and Zsa-Zsa -- straightened up in their seats, like school kids used to when the teacher entered the room. Here was the real deal. The man. Royalty, in their world.

Cobb, in turn, acknowledged each of them graciously, his half-smile suggesting that he might have something in mind. Evidently, while waiting in the green room, he had been watching the show with more interest than one might have expected.

He turned to Zsa-Zsa and said, "You know, Miss Gabor, I was wondering . . . when you told us . . . " -- picking up on something she had said earlier.

Zsa-Zsa remembered and appreciated the opportunity to clarify what she really meant to say.

Joey came up with a clever observation -- not nasty, just sharp. Johnny topped him, though not with a zinger, which wouldn't have worked anyway -- as he well knew -- in Cobb's presence.

Smart talk, from two fast and funny guys.

Lee laughed out loud, and so did Zsa-Zsa.

Cobb asked another question, again based on what had been said before he came out. And another. Keeping it moving. Stark and I couldn't get over it. A party was in full swing -- a real one -- *with Lee J. Cobb as its host!*

Indeed, it was great seeing Carson relaxed and enjoying himself. Even dour Joey was heard to chuckle. And Zsa-Zsa loved the attention she was getting from the courtly Cobb, who treated her in a courteous and respectful manner from the moment he entered the fray.

The rest of the time flew by.

When the show ended, nobody wanted to leave. Including me.

I thanked Lee for what had been a truly memorable evening.

BACK IN NEW YORK, I PRE-INTERVIEWED Woody Allen. He seemed out of sorts, conveying a lack of focus and often giggling inappropriately. He wasn't interested in talking about anything we considered. Including his new movie.

It was almost as if he was there under protest.

But when he took out a deck of playing cards and suggested he and Johnny might do a few card tricks, I felt better. Carson had started in the business doing magic but had never done any on the show.

Woody shuffled the deck in a highly professional manner, cut 'em a couple of times, and then did a "waterfall" shuffle, the cards accidentally spilling to the floor. He chortled. "Yeah, let's do that." Keep it in the act.

I thought that was a terrible idea and said so -- deferentially: Who was I to challenge Woody Allen when it came to comedy? But the charm of the spot would lie in the two funny men playing it straight, even earnestly.

Woody did it on the show, anyway, cards flying all over the place, the whole bit falling apart with them, Allen the only one laughing.

It was an act of schoolboy disdain.

If he hadn't wanted to do the show, he shouldn't have come on in the first place.

OVER THE TRANSOM ONE DAY CAME A MISSIVE from England.

It contained newspaper clippings and reprints of articles attesting to the existence of one Maurice Woodruff, reputed to be a seer of remarkable powers and impeccable credentials. The seventh son of a seventh son, his mother was a gypsy, and a seer herself.

More impressive, Peter Sellers, the gifted comic actor, allegedly reposed great confidence in him and was quoted as saying that he "never made a move" -- on career decisions, in contract negotiations, and the like -- "without talking to Maurice first."

Woodruff was due in the States shortly and would call, upon his arrival. I interviewed him soon thereafter.

He was a short, compactly built man, with a florid complexion, who exuded great energy and good humor, and marveled at his own gifts, being able to "see" what others could not, even as a child. He told me he gave readings to a few people, for which he charged fifty dollars -- a very low figure, even in those days, although perhaps not to an Englishman. At the end of the interview, he offered to do one for me, gratis. Professional courtesy, if you will.

Woodruff's appearance on the show went very well.

He was comfortable with himself and quick on the uptake. And his habit of speaking veryfast, veryfast, which made him at times almost unintelligible, was taken as idiosyncratic and hence charming.

The British, dontcha know.

I remember he came up with some stuff on Johnny, characteristics to which only Carson could attest. That the host was basically shy, for example, which in fact Johnny always took every opportunity to affirm, whenever it came up, not unaware of the disparity in the way the world saw him and the way he really was.

Maurice also left us with a sealed envelope, to be opened only after the first of the year, five months away -- why the delay, I'm not sure; probably just to add some mystery, create a little suspense.

We honored his request.

It contained a single prediction, deemed so ridiculous as to be dismissed out of hand: President Lyndon Baines Johnson was not going to run for re-election. Only to have LBJ, a few months later, appear on television and unceremoniously take himself out of the race!

But it was when I went to see Woodruff for my individual reading, shortly after his appearance on the show, that things took an unexpected turn, one which I suppose I might have anticipated.

He was staying at a hotel on Park Avenue, whose look of shabby gentility didn't live up to its upscale address. Seedy, it was.

Greeting me warmly, he ordered tea and something -- crumpets, maybe -- and sat down directly opposite me, a small coffee table between us. He gave me a pad and pencil, for taking notes, and got right to it, enumerating with considerable accuracy various characteristics of mine that he had no way of knowing about.

One in particular: that I occasionally experienced, for no apparent reason, a sharp pain in and just above my left eye, true to this day. But that "insight" could be discounted easily enough. I might well have given it away, unconsciously, by squinting or by rubbing my eyes -- enough for Woodruff, a shrewd observer of human behavior, to come up with a lucky guess.

He also picked up on some of my insecurities, which frankly I thought I had done a better job of masking, and saw me coming into a substantial amount of money -- not very likely at NBC, those rat bastids.

All in all, a pretty impressive performance.

"So," he said, "shall we recapitulate?"

He indicated I should stand up, as did he, stepping around the coffee table, a move which brought him closer to me, I noted, and began to summarize his findings.

"Now, you're going to get a pain right *here*," he told me, clamping his right hand on the back of my left thigh.

I was startled.

"Really?" I said.

"Oh, yes," he said.

As he withdrew his hand, he allowed the back of it to rake my genital area. Knuckled my groin.

"Oh!" he exclaimed, running his words together. "You're very well hung. I thought I was well hung, but you're very well hung . . . " Giving me what could only be described as a meaningful glance, he stated emphatically: "*It wants to go in someone's mouth, you know!*"

His eyes boldly locked in on mine, as in a silent movie. His face was flushed, vermilion. He looked . . . *uncomfortable*, actually. Exposed.

Acting without conscious thought, more in response to some innate mechanism, I reached down and gathered up my raincoat -- black, with a crimson lining -- and draped it over my left forearm, letting it fall deliberately to mid-thigh. Lowering a curtain, in effect, signifying the show was over.

"It" wasn't going anywhere.

My host exhaled audibly: air hissing from a tire.

He appeared to be somewhat relieved; if his gambit wasn't going to work, always a possibility, better it should end like this. With his eyes pretty much averted, he walked me to the door. We shook hands and wished each other well. And that was that.

As if nothing untoward had happened.

Later, a good friend of mine, upon hearing the tale, dubbed Woodruff a "seersucker."

Indubitably.

ED McMAHON WAS SUDDENLY IN BIG FAT trouble -- the phrase Art's, one of his favorites. Worse, it appeared the announcer didn't know it.

One can only wonder why -- driven by private demons, possibly; out of deep and abiding frustration, certainly -- but more and more he had been going beyond his role as straight man to Johnny. Out of nowhere, he seemed unable to keep from asserting his own self, which upset (to say the least) the show's equilibrium, its comic *purpose*, and was also slowly but inexorably driving its host wild. And, from what any of us could tell, being totally unaware of what he was doing, oblivious to its consequences.

Most, though not all, of his misbehavior showed up in the all-important segment at the desk between the two of them, immediately following the monologue. That's where Carson, wearing a lumpy turban that teetered precariously on his head, became "Carnac, the Magnificent," who, like Steve Allen's "Answer Man," gave the answers to questions before they were asked. Or the nattering "Aunt Blabby," reminiscent of "Maud Frickert," one of the great Jonathan Winters's earlier incarnations. Every night, something different, on a rotating basis.

The segment allowed Johnny to maintain the spirit and momentum of the monologue, and provided a nice bridge to what was to follow, when the guests came marching in.

Ed's errant behavior began innocently enough.

Johnny was setting up a particular piece of new business, whose basic premise, naturally, had to be clearly understood by the audience for it to work. It was never that complicated: a few, quick brush strokes, with McMahon underlining the central elements, and the job was done.

On this night, the set-up firmly in place, and with Johnny about to speak, Ed unexpectedly and vigorously re-stated the basic premise.

Carson's head swiveled.

He eyed his announcer balefully.

McMahon giggled and said weakly, "I just wanted to be sure I got it right . . . "

Johnny gave him a wan smile and the audience a fixed stare -- "the look." This was the kind of thing he had to put up with, what're you gonna do? (Carson never suffered fools gladly. His audiences loved it.)

The next time the bit was done, with Johnny's mouth agape, Ed re-stated the basic premise again. Twice.

And then, on another night, Ed did it again . . . and again . . . and a *third* time -- everyone in the studio, primed by this time, breaking up each step of the way. The announcer joined in the laughter, too -- reluctantly, as if in spite of himself. It *was* comical, one guy in effect not letting another guy speak. The host, in turn, had little choice but to go along with the gag, doing a long, and rather convincing, slow burn.

Stark told me later that Carson was very upset. Very. And like the rest of us, unable to comprehend what was happening.

Next, Ed took to challenging the basic premise, itself, "discussing" it with Johnny. This usually led to an unexpected colloquy between the two, for which Carson was completely unprepared. His ineffectual attempts to explain what he was trying to say -- even as, at the same time, he was unable to resist exploiting the situation's risible possibilities -- provoked much laughter.

Unfortunately, it was basically at his expense.

In private, I heard, Johnny was really starting to boil.

Generally, Ed did not know in advance the specifics of what was going to happen in any given segment, so as to insure that his reactions would be fresh and spontaneous. Whatever the concept, he was usually able to figure out where Carson was heading. Had he ever been tempted to speak out of turn, he had always resisted it.

Now, he started jumping in ahead of Johnny with the punch lines -- right on the nose, sometimes, or very much like what Carson had in mind. Leaving the star, more than once, with egg on his face.

Not a good idea.

Big Ed was acting loony. And Carson was now livid, according to Stark.

Yet, he never spoke directly to Ed about it.

The absence of a rebuke, of *some* kind of reaction from Johnny, must have added to McMahon's giddy state of mind. While Art, presumably, was expecting, or at least hoping, that it might yet happen. Or that Ed would, on his own, come to his senses, and the whole thing would just go away.

But then McMahon started making observations -- often, very amusing ones -- when Johnny was interviewing a guest. *His* guest. *Oy!*

The last straw came when the two were at the desk, following the monologue. Johnny was reading bits and pieces from the news and making funny comments about them. One, in particular, caught his eye. Scientists, he said, had proved conclusively that mosquitoes were attracted to sexy people. Johnny agreed. "That's right, they are." But before he could slap his wrist, "proving" it, Ed loudly slapped *his* wrist, beating Johnny to the punch. Leaving the host, his hand still raised, staring at his announcer in disbelief, McMahon, in turn, looking astonished at his own audacity, even as he laughed.

That did it.

Carson could take it no longer.

He was on the verge of firing his long-time associate.

Stark and I were in the producer's office, alone. It was mid-morning. Art looked visibly distressed.

I said, "Do you want me to talk to him?"

He considered it. "Would you?"

I nodded. "Sure."

"Okay."

Standing by the door to my office, while waiting for Ed to arrive, I thought about the exchange. Stark was not one to shy away from his responsibilities, however onerous. Nor did he avoid confrontations; on the contrary, it seemed at times almost as if he provoked them.

But since he was evidently so angry he "couldn't see straight" -- another favorite phrase -- he was concerned (I believe) that a talk with McMahon would inevitably turn into a scolding, a real dressing down, or worse. Ed had been with him for more than six years -- four, on *Who Do You Trust?*, and, by now, a couple of years on the *Tonight Show*. I think he felt the guy deserved better than that.

If, however, McMahon could find out the facts of life by himself, Stark was certain he would undoubtedly do what needed to be done, to ameliorate the situation.

Mine, hopefully, was to be the unseen hand that would bring this about.

When Ed appeared, I moseyed over to him and asked if he had a minute. He took a large sip from what was probably his first cup of coffee of the day, and made like Jackie Gleason: "How sweet it is!" -- everybody's favorite phrase, in those days. To me, he said: "What's up?"

I beckoned him to follow me and ushered him into my office. I closed the door and indicated he should sit down. Then, I buzzed my secretary, Gloria, and told her to hold my calls. A bit much, admittedly -- this wasn't a movie -- but it got his attention.

Without further ado -- without any ado -- I said, "Ed, you're in big, fat trouble. And I don't think you know it."

"Oh?" he said.

"Yes."

I proceeded to lay it all out for him, chapter and verse. He blanched, but listened attentively, his eyes never off the floor in front of him. His hand was steady, I was glad to see, the several times he brought his cup to his lips.

When I finished, I said, "Sorry, old buddy. But *some*body had to tell you . . . "

"Oh, no, no, no," he quickly replied. "I'm glad you did. I really appreciate it."

He rose and so did I.

We shook hands solemnly.

"Thank you," he said. "I mean it."

He took a deep breath and left, heading downstairs, straight to Johnny's office, where evidently the two had a long, *long* talk.

The rest is history.

Ed got back to being his usual hearty self and remained for all of Carson's lengthy run.

Interestingly, *our* relationship, such as it was, was never quite the same during the rest of my stay on the show. Not markedly different, but his comfort level with me appeared to be somewhat less than it had been before. Which is what can happen, I suppose, when bad tidings are conveyed, no matter how welcome, under the circumstances, those tidings might be.

TO UNDERSTAND JOHNNY CARSON, YOU HAVE to fully appreciate the impact hosting the *Tonight Show* had on him.

A naif from Nebraska, he found New York an alien place, full of supremely confident, fast-talking guys, the women perhaps a little too attractive, with sharp, knowing tongues, incomparably sure of *them*selves.

He may have been intimidated; he *was* intimidated.

But not when he was doing the show, with its controlled, nearly hermetic environment. There, he was at the top of his game -- most poised, most charming . . . most *interesting*. (Didn't David Letterman once say he *lived* for the one hour he did his show? The most intense, exciting, rewarding time of his day?) What we all saw, night after night, was the best of Johnny Carson.

Under what other conditions could such an opportunity present itself?

It was all a bit of a sham of course, as he well knew. A guilty pleasure, which, surprisingly, he'd sometimes acknowledge. On those infrequent occasions when the muse failed him and he was unable to come up with the kind of felicitous remark ("Frontier *bris!*") with which he was identified, he'd say, "Oh, if only my writers were here . . . " -- the line originally Jack Benny's, one of Carson's icons. (Red Skelton was another.) Letting the audience in on it. Making the point that the success he was having wasn't entirely deserved, if you only knew . . .

The fact that the comment was funny, in and of itself, and engaging, even ingratiating . . . that it evoked empathy and strengthened the connection between him and his audience . . . was a bonus, the rewards of his keen sense of showmanship.

I believe he *had* to say something, in order to placate his forebears and uphold the values they bestowed upon him. Probity. Playing it straight with other people . . .

And never telling a lie, except when it was, you know -- absolutely necessary.

His only difficult moments occurred during the commercial breaks, when he was faced with the awkward task (for him) of chatting companionably with his guest, trapped in the swivel chair.

What he would do was make a great show of looking busy, going over material long since absorbed. (Johnny was astonishingly quick at taking in whatever he was given.) Anything, it seemed, to keep from having to communicate with someone else, in what was an *un*controlled environment -- so different from the way it had been only moments ago, before going to commercial, and soon would be again when we came back.

But not soon enough.

(Our sympathies were usually with the guest. Stark, to me: "How'd *you* like to have to look into those cold blue eyes?")

To ease the tension, the responsibility his, after all, Johnny -- at last -- spoke to his guest. In funny. To exaggerated, and relieved, laughter. Turning yet again to his inordinate capacity to make people laugh, in order to get out of a sticky situation.

How come his interviews often worked, despite his conspicuous lack of interviewing skills?

Because, I would guess, the danger inherent in his monologues *carried over* to his interviews, the hammer not dropping that often, but there was always the possibility that it might. (The expectation was there.) Let the guest stumble just a little bit, look a little foolish, and Johnny might well swoop in. Saying nothing, while giving his audience "the look," the one many of them were waiting for. Praying for.

Then, screams.

That, and the enormous acceptance his fans tendered him.

His interviews failing to cut the mustard probably reinforced the notion that their host was really one of them.

So, he wasn't perfect.

Neither were they; not really.

However it came to pass, Johnny's thirty-year reign as Americas' #1 talk show host, particularly considering how little his natural disposition for the task -- distant by predilection, not by choice -- has to be one of the most remarkable achievements in the history of the game.

SHE WAS YOUNG AND ATTRACTIVE, MORE handsome than beautiful, I'd say, but it was a close call. She had a warm and ready, dimpled smile and her brown-button eyes seemed to take in everything.

She was there to see me about a book she had written, a coffee-table number -- its cover a bright, pinkish color, I remember -- about fun and games at the beach. ("The Beach Book," published the same year that Betty Friedan came out with "The Feminine Mystique.") Her publisher, what with summer coming on, thought that it and she were a natural for the show.

Maybe so.

There was more to her than that.

Earlier, she had been a Bunny at one of the Playboy clubs, getting the lowdown from the inside on the famous nightclub. All of what she uncovered appeared, no holds barred, in an article she subsequently wrote for Esquire magazine.

That was a natural for the show.

Her name was Gloria Steinem.

In her first segment, she talked about the book and revealed how clever she was. "A landing party from Aristotle Onassis' yacht has just come ashore to ask you to join them. You say no." Completely relaxed, she appeared to be enjoying herself.

Johnny liked her. Which probably meant the audience did, too.

In her second segment, she went into what was going on at the Playboy Club, where evidently things were not what they appeared to be.

It was, as she saw it, a highly exploitative enterprise, the "girls" overworked and underpaid, while being compelled to adhere to an exacting, almost puritanical, code of conduct. At the same time, they had to put up with the endless ogling and heavy-handed banter that came their way from the hot shots they were serving.

She also talked about the "Bunny Dip," the prescribed manner drinks were to be served, never by bending over even a little bit -- which might stir the boys up *too* much -- but dipping at the knees, so as to remain upright at all times.

Such a vertical movement left the Bunny able to reach the table only by extending her arm -- drink in hand -- in an extremely awkward motion that often left her teetering, like Carnac's turban, while constantly struggling to maintain her balance.

Some fun!

I believe Gloria also gave a demonstration of the "Bunny Dip," which may be an instance of memory-turned-fantasy. Looking back, I "see" her in a Bunny costume, with a lot of décolletage, decorously defying gravity . . .

In any case, that this was an indelible experience in her life seems likely. Indeed, it may have been the trigger that spurred her later into leading the charge for women's rights in this country, though, of course, there was more to it than that.

Rights to Ms. Steinem's story were sold to the movies. The film starred Kirstie Alley.

THE TIME HAD COME FOR ME TO PETITION NBC for an increase in salary, which hadn't moved an inch since the day I was hired.

I also wanted the title "Associate Producer," and I wanted it badly -- the kind of thing you look back on and wonder what all the fuss was about. But I hoped to be a producer when I grew up, and this was a mandatory first step.

Besides, I deserved it.

With Art and Johnny's support, I made my move.

NBC took its own sweet time in making a decision -- understandably, this being a matter of such gravity.

Finally, they approved the new title, *and* a raise -- a fabulous twenty-five dollars, which kicked my salary up to a stratospheric $250 a week. Not, as previously noted, a lot of money even in those days.

The fact is, it was a goddam insult.

NBC: Long on titles -- I was now "Associate Producer & Head Talent Coordinator" -- and short on bread.

I turned it down, the raise, in a quixotic gesture that I regret to this day.

Not, really. Yes, really.

Rat bastids.

JAMES COBURN, WHOSE FINE WORK HAD BEEN consistently overlooked or taken for granted by the critics, I believe (at least until his recent Academy Award), did the show one night. He was genuinely excited about it, eager as a puppy, and his appearance went well. Nothing special, to be sure, except that he closed it out by playing . . . the gong!

Lovingly. His very own, a beautiful, ornate, Oriental gong. Quite sizable -- at least a yard in diameter.

There he was, Mrs. Coburn's son, Jim, tall and angular, down on one knee in front of the desk, banging away at his instrument with a soft mallet -- one booming, resonating note after another. Concentrating on it; working at it; suddenly aware of his intensity and breaking into a broad grin. But back in haste to his "music."

Having a wonderful time.

Don Rickles was there, missing the point. Falling apart, as if he couldn't believe it: "A *gong!*"

Oh, to be secure enough to be able to do something outré, not as a convention-flouting gesture but simply because it gave you joy. Braving the eye-rolling and the ridicule, and genuinely not caring an i-o-ta about either.

Coburn, in a world of his own, was *happy*.

AH, RICKLES.

The *chutzpah* king.

The first time he did the show, it never occurred to any of us that he would do his put-down number on Johnny. Or on anybody else who was out there with him.

I mean, not "live."

At that point, we knew of him only by reputation, which was admittedly spreading like one of those blazes in the Hollywood Hills, an irresistible force, zigzagging up the side of a mountain.

Principally, though, I think it was because the idea just seemed . . . un*seemly*. To make the host look bad. We weren't ready for that, even if, as was being said, those he dumped on -- particularly celebrities -- *loved* it, couldn't get enough of it, the more they got bopped, the better. Leading the laughter . . .

But here, in front of everybody -- the studio audience, and the one at home?

Uh-uh.

Not to mention the subterranean question: How would Johnny handle it?

No, no. Too risky. Maybe that's what was happening in other places, to other people. But not to us. Not to our peerless leader.

So, when I pre-interviewed Don, it was a given, as far as we were concerned. I told him that he could talk *about* what he did, and give examples, but not actually do his thing on the show. Impervious to his frown, though registering it subliminally, I grandly assumed that since we felt that way, he would too; the whole *world* would see it as we did -- the *Tonight Show* audience, for sure.

Thus, Rickles wound up relating the signal episode of his career, to that point. The one everybody in the business was talking about.

It was Rickles's practice, in his nightclub act, to end his ongoing, and often very clever -- even witty -- onslaughts with a mini-sermon, an explanation that what he had been doing was all in fun, just kidding, he hoped no one had taken offense, he certainly didn't mean it that way. Now that the fun and games were over, wasn't it marvelous that we were all still good friends?

We *were* still good friends, weren't we?

(Applause, applause, applause.)

Evidently, at one of his shows, he stopped his act abruptly and drew the audience's attention to the fact that at a table only a few feet in front of him sat three gentlemen in Arab garb -- robes and burnooses, the whole bit. And here he was, a Jewish guy, which he made no bones about -- not exactly impartial when it came to the Arab-Israeli conflict. But this was America, and wasn't it great that we could all live together and get along so nicely, blah, blah, blah.

This peroration elicited only mild applause, until a spotlight hit the three guys. The clapping firmed up immediately and began to build.

Rickles helped.

"Gentleman, please," he said, gesturing. "Stand up and take a bow."

The Arabs looked at one another, trapped and not fully understanding why. Stand up and take a bow? What was this fool babbling about?

"No, seriously. Please," Don persisted. "Take a bow."

The audience joined in, registering some irritation.

"Stand up! Come on, take a bow, already!"

Tentatively, glancing about them, with uncertain grins on their faces, the three slowly began to rise.

To thunderous applause.

Only in America.

Now, the visitors from the Middle East were on their feet, bowing and preening at all that good will coming their way.

Rickles joined in the applause.

"Wonderful! Wonderful!" he said.

Then, stepping back, he cupped his hands to his mouth, and shouted:

"OPEN FIRE!"

It took a beat for the line to register. Less than a beat. Followed by whoops and hollers! And wild, rollicking laughter, everyone immediately flashing on someone they couldn't wait to tell about what had just happened.

Shaking their heads.

"OPEN FIRE!"

The things that guy comes up with.

Pretty much from that point on, Rickles was Rickles, on the show -- going after everybody, Johnny included. We all loved it, but the studio audience's reaction, the first few times was -- well, okay, but not nearly as enthusiastic as ours.

It occurred to me that it might be a good idea for Rickles, when he made his entrance, to lay off Carson for a bit. Give the audience a chance to get used to what he was doing. It was all right to pick on Ed and on Skitch. After Johnny broke up -- which was bound to happen -- *then*, Don could bop him at will.

Rickles listened to what I was saying with an intensity I had never encountered before. Once he was out there, he did almost exactly everything I had suggested. The audience, seeing Johnny laughing at what was happening to McMahon and Henderson, and how he screamed when *he* was the target, realized it was okay for them to laugh, as well.

They sat back and enjoyed the mayhem.

It was not that hard to figure out why some audiences loved Rickles. It's always great fun to see the mighty taken down -- as happened in Carson's monologues, as well. Nor is it difficult to understand those who were put off by his sheer effrontery, his thumbing his nose at normal, societal constraints.

Often, the two contradictory responses overlapped, people finding him funny as hell, one minute; that he had gone too far, the next.

The question that was harder to answer was, Why did celebrities, the *objects* of his skewerings, go along with it? What kind of madness was this?

Well, for one thing, the fact that Don had singled them out reinforced the notion that they were special, part of an elite group. You must really be somebody to merit that kind of abuse.

And since you took it so well, not only laughing but cracking up over the beating you were getting, you had demonstrated in a praiseworthy fashion what a good sport you were.

More important, perhaps, the experience gave you an opportunity to shrug off, at least for a little while, the terrible burden of celebrityhood, which half the time you weren't that sure you really deserved, anyway. In that moment of "humiliation," you were exposed, warts and all. Humanized. And the world hadn't come to an end.

However it came to pass, from the beginning of Don's rapid rise, it has been considered a badge of honor to have him hand your head to you.

Still is, I believe.

Rickles, for whom one has a sneaking admiration, does what we'd all like to do, at least just once, without fear or favor.

MAYBE WE SHOULDN'T BE SURPRISED AT HIS success.

103

"Kill the people!"

That's what Thelma Ritter says to Bette Davis -- not meaning it literally, we can assume -- in the movie, *All About Eve*, as Margo Channing (Miss Davis) is about to go on stage.

Performers "at war" with their audience is a familiar metaphor. What happens sometimes is as much a battle as it is a performance. The audience not only has to be won over, but vanquished.

If the notion applies to any particular group, it has to be stand-up comics. What do they deliver, time and again? Punch lines: Pow! (Maybe that's why they behave so oddly, at times; they're punch drunk.)

Take two gentlemen who did our show fairly frequently -- Milt Kamen and, for a while, Murray Roman.

Kamen's first appearances at the stand-up game were at clubs in Manhattan, like The Blue Angel and Bon Soir, which catered to a sophisticated clientele. In a special piece of material, he admits to being both bedeviled and intimidated by all the talk about Brooks Brothers, the exclusive men's clothing store. He decides to give it a try, though it is clearly uncharted, possibly alien, territory.

Once he starts discarding his old wardrobe, however, replacing it piece by piece with one of the store's classically traditional outfits, he undergoes a remarkable change.

His eyes begin to sparkle . . .

A knowing smile plays about his lips . . .

He feels . . . *taller*.

The makeover complete, he finds himself "humming in French."

The audience recognizes who Kamen is satirizing: themselves. But doing it well. Tastefully. And being funny, in the process.

By the time he made it to the *Tonight Show*, he had modified his act -- more a returning to his basic moorings. Now, he was less the urban sophisticate, and more the sharp observer of the passing scene -- with a Jewish sensibility. And when he hit upon the device of reviewing movies -- as an inventive, sometimes phantasmagorical, always dyspeptic critic -- he became an occasional regular on the show.

Here, approximately, is how he wrapped-up his review of *Hamlet*:

"Hamlet's father returns, which surprises everybody, since he's been dead from even before the movie started. His own brother, Claudius, murdered him. Oh, yeah . . .

"Claudius is now married to Hamlet's mother, Gertrude. She died by mistake, earlier. Poisoned. It wasn't on purpose. I don't know; something must have gone wrong . . .

"Anyway, the old man looks at all those dead bodies -- Gertrude's . . . Hamlet's . . . and what's-his-name, Ophelia's brother -- him too. Ophelia was Hamlet's girl friend. She was crazy, altogether.

"Hamlet's father is not very happy, which, you know, can't come as a complete surprise, under the circumstances.

"'Go,' he says to the world, shaking his head dolefully, 'try and raise a family.'"

Milt laughed, ahead of the audience by a fraction of a second. Making sure they "got" it, that he was only kidding. Bit of a cheat, that. Others do it, as well.

Kamen also made occasional appearances on Broadway, in small, at times multiple character parts. In Paddy Chayefsky's play, *The Passion Of Joseph D.*, he had two such roles, neither of any significance.

Yet, though the play only got respectable notices, his overall performance was singled out by some of the reviewers. He had probably overacted, or done something close to outrageous in order to draw attention to himself, not uncommon among comics turned legit. (By the time I got to see Zero Mostel, in *Fiddler on the Roof*, it had been running six months. The great actor kept inserting his own shtick into his performance, appearing to be more Zero than Tevya, the one bearing little resemblance to the other.)

Milt was due for our pre-interview, as it happened, the morning after the play opened. He walked into my office looking agitated and unhappy.

"Did you see my reviews?" he asked me, not waiting for an answer. "That Chayefsky! You think Jerry Lewis has an ego? Fuhgetaboutit!"

"Oh?" I said.

"Oh, yeah!"

It seemed that Milt had been complaining all along that his parts had been underwritten -- from the standpoint of the play, he would piously insist. Soon after the curtain came down, as he told it, Chayefsky came over and conceded that Kamen had been right.

"'I'm going to rewrite both your parts,' he said. 'Give you more to say. You know, like we discussed . . . '" Milt's eyes glittered. "I said to him, 'No, you're not!' He said, 'I'm not?' 'No!' I said. *'I'm going to rewrite 'em!'* Paddy looked at me like he couldn't believe his ears. 'All right,' he said to me, finally. 'You do it.'"

The comic, his face aglow, looked triumphant.

I didn't get it.

The theater is a playwright's medium. Not a word can be changed without his approval. Did he honestly expect me to believe that Paddy Chayefsky, one of the most respected figures in the theater, had actually gone along with this *mishugas?*

On the other hand, the whole exchange was so bizarre there might have been some truth to it.

Most likely it was Kamen, not Chayefsky, who had brought the matter up, after the curtain came down. The exhausted playwright was probably not disposed to do battle then and there, particularly with a lesser player. In the re-telling, as might have been expected, the whole thing took on this quality of sheer fantasy. With Milt appearing to believe it happened exactly as he told it.

Oh, well.

I offered him a cup of coffee, and we got started on the pre-interview.

For a short time, Murray Roman -- sharply jagged features, made more prominent by the heavy black, horn-rimmed glasses he wore, which somehow managed to make his eyes always look moist -- also reviewed movies for us, in the wickedly sardonic mode.

Murray was a talker, a *schmoozer* -- the kind Lee Cobb had insisted he was not. An amiable smart-ass, fun to have around at a party, of the kind we had in mind (in a way) for Johnny to host every night.

The problem, doctor, was that he was a talker offstage, as well. And once he started, he couldn't stop. It apparently never even *occurred* to him to knock it off.

At one taping, five minutes before air time, I looked around, and no Murray. Not in the Green Room, with the other guests, nor in the men's room.

Where the hell was he?

Then, I spotted him backstage, with Johnny, talking, talking, talking, his mouth at no time further than six inches away from Carson's ear, no matter which way the gentleman from Nebraska turned. Those few moments before the start of the show were precious, Johnny's own -- to have a smoke and settle himself down. No one had ever disturbed him during that period before.

"Murray!" I hissed.

Roman froze and instantly grasped the inappropriateness of what he was doing. He pulled away from Carson just as the *Tonight Show* theme was starting up, and hustled over to me.

"I'm sorry, man," he said, looking like he was about to cry, although you couldn't really tell, with those glasses. "I mean it, man. I really am."

I was about to cry.

On another occasion, he was having dinner with his manager, Ray (not his real name), and Ray's wife, Fay (nor hers), at their house. Over dessert and coffee, and feeling quite expansive, Murray assured Fay that she didn't have to worry any more. Ray was through with that girl he'd been seeing.

"He told me so, himself."

Fay had been unaware of her husband's dalliance. Stricken, she got up and left the room.

Roman glanced at his manager, and from the beleaguered look on his face realized he had screwed up again.

"Jesus, man!" the comic said. "I'm sorry. I really am."

As I'm sure he was. Truly sorry.

I mean, how can you hate a guy like that?

Easy.

ON THE OTHER HAND, THERE WERE TWO comics with whom I had some contact that were hard *not* to like.

Henny Youngman sometimes came to my office and used my phone to call his writer in California, to get material for his next appearance on the show.

"You don't mind, do you?"

While listening, he'd laugh, repeating the jokes aloud, as he heard them -- gauging my reaction, his only audience. And, truth to tell, probably not getting an accurate picture from me. I laughed at everything his man on the Coast, an unsung hero, came up with.

The one joke I remember hearing -- before anybody else, which made me feel as if, in some way, I was in on its inception -- was about the doctor who tells his patient he has only six months to live.

"I demand a second opinion," the patient says.

"All right," the doctor tells him, "you're ugly, too."

Henny's humor was essentially gentle and benign. His jokes cut occasionally, as in the above, but never too deeply.

"Take my wife -- please!"

The fact is he didn't have a mean bone in his big, shambling body.

Another likeable guy was Morey Amsterdam, who played Buddy, one of the comedy writers on the old *Dick Van Dyke Show*, the best of the early television

109

situation comedies. Quick and funny he appeared on the *Tonight Show* only once or twice but became a regular on a syndicated talk show I produced, after Carson let me go.

Driving west on Hollywood Blvd. one day, I noticed a large sign -- more, a small billboard -- that I hadn't seen before. It just had two words on it, in big letters. I pointed it out to Morey and said the words aloud: "Jesus Saves."

"Yeah," said Amsterdam slyly, "but Moses Invests."

Both gentlemen expressed uniquely Jewish sensibilities.

One, which informed all of Henny's material, was the notion that we are all a little foolish, at times, and all too often tend to take ourselves too seriously, but don't worry about it, life goes on no matter what we do.

Might as well enjoy.

Another, evident in Morey's quip, was that Jews tend to feel they can always, even routinely, outsmart most Gentiles. They like the feeling. It has provided them with considerable emotional sustenance through the years, when in fact their very existence sometimes depended upon their ability to outwit those who would do them harm.

Jews are not alone.

I'm certain that Blacks make lots of jokes in which they are more clever than whites. A lot more. As do others, against those they resent, or fear, for real or perceived reasons.

Perhaps the lesson is, if it's funny, give it voice. Laughter is a cleansing agent. And if a few feathers are ruffled along the way, so be it. So long as you're not being mean-spirited about it, using humor as a weapon. Not *too* mean-spirited, anyway.

There is at least one other thing a Jewish comic has to deal with: his anger.

Which brings us back to Don Rickles.

THE *TONIGHT SHOW*, STARRING JOHNNY Carson, was now moving along, singing a song. Night after night, we were putting out first-rate shows, and feeling pretty damned good about it.

Our way was very different from that of Johnny's predecessor, the mercurial Jack Paar. He'd present a week's worth of rather just-okay shows -- his persona always the dominant element, in any case -- and then come up with a spectacular outing that'd carry him for a month.

There was one night where Paar had *five* comics on, Shelly Berman and Jonathan Winters among them. They literally took over, Jack looking aggrieved but resigned. He wound up surrendering his place at the desk to his guests, who then interviewed each other, using Paar's notes, before ostentatiously crumpling them up and throwing them away. By that time, Jack was stretched out in one of the set's alcoves, up on one elbow, framed against a reproduction of the Manhattan skyline . . . and the hell with it!

Those kinds of chances we didn't take.

If we had five comics available to us, we'd space them out, one per night, trading off one possible gangbusters show for five very likely good ones.

Ed McMahon was back on board, the tensions between host and announcer a distant memory. He and Johnny worked together better than ever.

To Carson's "Carnac, the Magnificent," Ed made a small addition, much as he had with "*How . . . cold . . . was . . . it?*" in the monologue.

When "Carnac" stated the answer to the as-yet undetermined question, Ed repeated it, in a strong clear voice, an act disturbingly reminiscent of what he had done during his mixed-up days. But here the intent was clearly in the spirit of the thing.

"Carnac," who had already begun to open the envelope which contained the question, reacted as if he had heard -- what? An echo? It certainly seemed like it. But where had it come from???

Looking all about him -- up, down and around -- his gaze finally settled on Ed.

"Oh!" he said, as if startled. "It was you!"

His turban teetered.

McMahon, no longer able to keep from laughing, acknowledged that it was he.

This make-believe miscommunication between the two never missed, and was repeated often, with variations. "Carnac": "Did you hear something?" Ed: "I think it was an echo . . . " Johnny either keeping it going -- "An echo? Hard to believe, somehow . . . " -- or rolling his eyes and tearing open the envelope, which he always blew into, to puff it up, the easier to extract the card that had the question on it. All of this not so much a performance as an informal, light-hearted exchange between two guys just goofing around, its tone characterizing much of what was happening on the show, which had clearly hit its stride.

But success is not without its consequences.

Everywhere Johnny went, people kept telling him how amazed they were at his durability.

"Jesus Johnny, I don't know how you do it. Night after night . . . " They were insistent about it, later telling their friends and acquaintances, "I was talking to Carson the other day, and I said to him . . . "

After a while, Johnny began to believe it.

Most performers tend to feel put-upon, anyway. Under appreciated. On our show, the workload *was* heavy -- an hour-and-a-half, five nights a week, the pressure constant, the grind seemingly endless.

Who needs it?

Besides, while it was fine to knock 'em dead in late-night, you weren't really a star until you had made it in *prime time*.

What he ought to be doing, Carson became convinced, was a once-a-week show, like everybody else. One that would air at, say, 10PM. Late night, but still *prime time.*

Yeah!

That'd do it!

Johnny's contract, it so happened, was up for renewal.

Intrepidly, he contacted his attorneys. After "heavy confabs," they notified NBC that their client did not intend to stay on as host of the *Tonight Show*, opting instead for a spot in (*yes!*) prime time -- at which, naturally, NBC would have first crack.

A hurried search for a replacement was quickly set in motion.

He wasn't the only one who felt put-upon and under-appreciated.

So did the talent coordinators.

Booking was a lot harder than it looked, the show a giant maw that chewed up guests like so many M&Ms. Fifteen a week, week after week.

At any given moment, we'd be set for that night's taping, to be sure, and probably the next two nights as well, but there was still a hole, maybe more than one, in the show after that. And in the one after *that* we might be waiting for confirmation on a major star, around whom the other bookings would revolve. Our intention was to orchestrate each show's lineup, whenever we could, as to make the *groupings* sound inviting, even though each guest in fact rose or fell pretty much on his or her own.

But what if the major star we hadn't yet heard from fell out? There had to be a backup plan in place, and more than one. "If she can't make it, we can move him into that slot, and shift *her* over to here. Or, if necessary . . . " While, at that same given moment, having only partial bookings set for the *next* night after that, and just a few for the following week.

And the process itself was, at best, uneven.

Sometimes, there was a profusion of available guests; on other days, hardly any -- high-caliber ones, that is. But even amid the plenty, there were always random spots that still needed to be filled, before we could finally complete a particular night's menu. Moving more guests around, if necessary, which we didn't like to do.

On and on, without letup.

Now, with the show doing so well, what we were foolishly concerned about was that everybody would assume we were practically on automatic pilot. That all we had to do was sit back and pick and choose.

Not true.

(It was never true!)

This was a hard concept to get across to others, without sounding as if we were feeling sorry for ourselves. Like we were ingrates, or something. Woe unto those who feel themselves misunderstood.

I mused about it aloud one day, in the middle of a booking session. Just sounding off.

"If people only knew how really tough this is, they'd --"

"No!" thundered Stark, unexpectedly in high dudgeon. "They don't *have* to know! It's none of their concern! All they have to worry about is what they see, the show itself! Is it good or is it bad? That's all!"

He was right, of course, and I made a quick switch, a la Perry Cross.

"That's what I said. Nobody has to know how tough our job is." I waved my hand, dismissively. "All they're interested in is the product, what we give them. Everything else is irrelevant . . . "

The other bookers laughed.

Art didn't get it, at first; then he caught on, and smiled. More important, his color began to return to normal. "Exactly," he said, getting in the last word, to which he was entitled.

Other unworthy sentiments crowded in.

What do you mean, how did Carson do it, night after night? We did all the work, for crying out loud! Coming up with the guests. And doing the damn pre-interviews, without which ol' Johnny would be lost.

So we too were a little unhappy, even as we gloried in the show's success.

Go figure there'd be this much discontent on a show that had "clearly hit its stride."

HOLLYWOOD'S FAVORITE GURU, AT THE TIME, the Maharishi Mahesh Yogi, and the great surrealist artist, Salvador Dali, as well-known for his piercing stare as his marvelously drafted surreal paintings, vied -- in a contest too close to call -- for the most hard-to-understand guests we ever had, during the period that ran from October 1, 1962, to some time in April, the cruelest month, 1967.

The Maharishi, whom I was asked by the actress, Diane Baker, as a favor to "just have a chat with," proved to be a darling little man. Wrapped, inter*twined*, in a clean white sheet, he did nothing but beam and make a sound denoted in comic strips as "tee-hee" throughout our pre-interview, and on the show itself. So diminutive was he that he had to scramble like a toddler -- or so it seemed -- to get into his chair, there to assume the lotus position, as he tried to explain what the hell "TM" (Transcendental Meditation) was. Something to do with, as he kept repeating, the "t'ought," meaning the *thought*, I think, which traveled allegedly in a straight line from the head to the belly button. "It's the t'ought," he kept saying, with spirit. "The t'ought!"

116

He turned out to be a delightful guest -- though Art ended his interview after only one segment -- but I guarantee that nobody understood a word he had said.

It was worse with Dali, in a way, because he brought along his wife, Galina, to interpret for him, she, in turn, only slightly less unintelligible than her husband. Both spoke some kind of odd-sounding, Castillian dialect, so thick that, upon hearing, you couldn't believe even they understood it.

Two guests to confound the viewer, for the price of one.

What stands out in memory is Dali, a striking-looking character, with cape and cane, challenging the world through wide, popping eyes, coming across like nothing so much as a caricature of himself...

And the remarkably considerate way Carson handled both him, his wife and the Maharishi.

Old-fashioned, Midwestern gentility, which renders all other considerations -- going for laughs and charming (or is it appeasing?) the audience -- moot.*

PURLIE VICTORIUS, A COMEDY, STARRING Ossie Davis and Ruby Dee, opened on Broadway. They were (and are) husband and wife, two very talented black actors -- he, of the deep, resonating voice; she, simply lovely, in every way. Mr. Davis had written the play, which received enthusiastic notices.

I knew of them and urged Art to book them, which he did.

---

* It was this same heritage, I think, that always prompted Johnny to pull back from any act of his which could be perceived as excessive.

The pre-interview, with the three of us crowded into my tiny office, barely large enough for two -- astonishingly, still a source of irritation to this day! -- went beautifully. Both talked easily and well, and gave a demonstration of a short, self-contained moment from the play. It ran about three or four minutes, and was delightful.

I was certain they'd knock 'em dead on the show.

The next morning, the day before their scheduled appearance, Dave Tebet, a VP at NBC, the network's trouble-shooter and PR guy to the stars, paused at my door. Disposed to strut about and give orders, I rather liked him.

He said to me, in his terse, no-nonsense manner:

"Those two, Ossie Davis and Ruby Dee? They're out. Period."

I was stunned.

I couldn't believe it.

The look on my face must have registered, because he added:

"That's it! They're out!"

The only conceivable reason for their being dropped from the show had to be that they were still on one of those terrible "lists" of unacceptable, left-leaning performers that had flourished during the McCarthy era of the fifties and had cost many good people their livelihoods, and often much, much more.

But at this late date? In the mid-*sixties*?

I, along with everyone else, had assumed that that sort of thing no longer existed, where a handful of complaints against an artist could bring the networks to their knees, bowing without a struggle to the pressure and temper of the times.

My first reaction was to take a public stand against it, even as I realized what a futile gesture that would be. The two actors would still be cancelled, merely by someone else.

And I might be out, too.

I called *Purlie's* P.R. guy and apprised him of what had happened, unable to keep the distress out of my voice.

"Please tell Ossie and Ruby how sorry I am."

He said he would, of course.

After that, I contacted the Herald Tribune, then New York's other responsible morning newspaper. It had an able and aware TV department, which, surprisingly, the Times did not. I identified myself to the reporter who took the call and gave him the whole story, though I made it clear from the start -- rather, self-importantly, I fear -- that what I told him was not for attribution.

"I'll deny it, if you quote me directly," I said. "If you use my name, it'll probably cost me my job."

He agreed not to, and I unburdened myself. I was assured that the story would be in the next day's paper. After I hung up, I joined Art and the other talent coordinators to hustle up a replacement for our excommunicated guests.

The Herald Tribune gave it considerable coverage, but when NBC stonewalled, it wound up as only a two-, maybe three-day, affair.

And I never did hear from anybody "upstairs."

Dave Tebet must have known it was I who had contacted the Trib, but he probably figured it was best to leave it alone. NBC reprimanding me publicly would only have made matters worse.

Actually, in retrospect, I doubt if what I had done meant all that much to them, the big boys, one way or another.

THE SEARCH FOR A SUCCESSOR TO CARSON was still going on, with nobody worthy enough to replace him in sight.

But Johnny himself was beginning to have second thoughts.

In part, they were due to an understandable concern over giving up a known and well-functioning enterprise for a completely unknown one. Having to start all over again. Abandoning, in effect, a considerable investment in time and effort.

The very nature of the alternative underlined the risk he was about to take.

If there was an occasional bad show on *Tonight*, not to worry, we could always catch up with the next one, or the one after that. But two or three so-so appearances in prime time, all too possible during the period when the new show would be getting its legs under it, the critics waiting to pounce . . . and it could be all over.

Besides, and possibly more important, on a once-a-week show, what was Carson going to do with all that newly available free time? The way things were, he had *a place to go to* five days a week. (By Friday nights he looked forward to his weekends, *needing* the time off.) Not to mention that week-long torrent of applause he received with us, compared to only the one night's worth, doing what he had committed himself to.

The more Johnny thought about it, the less he liked his earlier decision, and the more he wanted out.

Art Stark sensed what was going on, though Carson never spoke directly to him about it, making only a few sardonic remarks along the way, speaking in a kind of code.

Johnny was clearly out on a limb, with too much "pride" to climb down off it.

Stark proceeded to make a luncheon date with two of NBC's top executives -- for no special reason, he told them, and with no specific agenda in mind. It was simply a good idea to get together, every once in a while, right? During the deadly meal, the laughter forced and too many drinks consumed by the gentlemen from the network, Art off-handedly inquired as to how the search for Carson's successor was going.

With the question, any pretense of bonhomie collapsed.

NBC was in a spot, the troubled executives admitted, and not at all sanguine about it. There was no one around even remotely in Johnny's league to take his place.

The producer made his move.

"You know, fellas," he said, as if ruminating aloud, "I have a feeling" -- he paused to add sweetener to his coffee -- "that if you guys were to ask Johnny" -- and took a sip -- "in a nice way, of course . . . " -- chuckling -- "it wouldn't surprise me . . . if he just might consider . . . *staying on . . .* as host of the show."

Shazam!

His two guests came alive. They thanked and thanked again their host, all but bowing down to him, and made their goodbyes in haste, heading straight for their offices.

After they left, Art nodded and called for the check. Then, he leaned back and smiled inwardly, looking like, I would think, nothing so much as a contented iguana, basking in the sun.

AS A RESULT OF HIS NEW CONTRACT, JOHNNY had seven weeks off in the summer, some of which he spent in Vegas with a nightclub act that proved to be very successful. Stark told me that much of it was a reprise of some of his *Tonight Show* shtick.

During this period his duties as host were covered by various players, the saturnine Joey Bishop getting most of the action. Bishop did well enough at it to get his own talk show later on ABC, which would air at 11:30 PM, in direct competition with the *Tonight Show*. Naturally.

Two of his shows with us -- no, three -- I remember very well.

The first time Frank Sinatra appeared with Joey, he brought along Dean Martin, unannounced, to cheers, whistles and wild applause. Bishop welcomed them both, Dean saying he was glad to be here, that bibulous manner he presumably affected leaving the impression that he might not be certain just where, exactly, "here" was. Within minutes, he and Frank gave a mini-demonstration of "rat pack" humor, with its patented air of comic disdain.

In the middle of an exchange with the host, they both suddenly flicked their cigarettes away, in high, roughly parallel arcs . . . shouted "Air Raid!" . . . and stuck fingers in their ears, ducking down in their seats, as if an explosion was imminent. Only to return to chatting with Bishop as before, making no reference to or acknowledging in any way what they had done.

It was outlandish if not childish behavior, although not without a certain charm. Insouciance, as a way of life.

In Frank's second appearance, Joey asked him about his new movie, *Assault On A Queen.*

"Yeah," Sinatra replied, straightforwardly enough, "it came out pretty good." Then, he volunteered:

"It's about three guys beating up Clifton Webb."

Webb, memorable as "Waldo Leidecker," in the classic film noir, *Laura*, was known among the West Coast cognoscenti to be homosexual.

As soon as the segment ended and we were into commercial, I saw Frank call Dave Tebet over and heard him say he wanted the line cut. Tebet, who was at the taping only because Sinatra was on the show, turned to me and said, peremptorily:

"I want that line *cut!*"

So did Art and I. The minute we heard Frank utter it, we knew it would have to go -- as, to his credit, did he.

I passed the command decision on to Bobby Quinn, the associate director, who took care of such matters. Millions of viewers were left wondering what Sinatra had said that was so wicked NBC felt they couldn't handle it.

Only in this instance, it wasn't the network that had made the determination to edit the tape.

It was ol' Blue Eyes, himself.

The great Phil Silvers, of "Sgt. Bilko" fame, made his only appearance on the *Tonight Show* with Joey.

He wasn't pre-interviewed by a talent coordinator. A phone call between him and the host, an old friend, would do the trick. Two pros, working it out between themselves, cutting out the middleman.

Silvers evidently told Joey he had a great story he wanted to tell. A true story.

"You'll love it. Trust me."

Bishop did, because it would have been rude not to -- an affront to his guest's dignity -- and anyway, why shouldn't he? Phil, as "Bilko," had been one of the funniest performers ever. Of course, when doing that show, and in his many other classically funny roles, he was reciting words others had written for him.

A talent coordinator would have wanted to hear the tale.

Silvers, who had heretofore resisted going on talk shows, was doing ours as a favor to Joey, who, we heard, had to talk him into it. All of us awaited his appearance with considerable anticipation.

Joey got right to it.

"Phil, you said you had an interesting story you wanted to share with the *Tonight Show* audience . . . "

Silvers brightened.

"Oh, yes."

The tale he proceeded to relate was thoroughly confusing from the start and didn't get any clearer the further he got into it. There were so many characters wandering in and out and so much going on that it was absolutely *impossible to follow*. And with Silvers presenting each element with such loving detail, such energy and enthusiasm, their failing to register made it all the harder to bear.

Joey deadpanned his distress a couple of times.

"But, Phil . . . "

"Wait! Wait!" Silvers assured him, indicating that everything would become clear soon enough, just be patient.

It never happened.

We were now into his second segment, Phil apparently oblivious to the impact -- the *non*-impact -- he was having on the studio audience, whose silence he must have assumed reflected rapt attention, the degree to how mesmerized it was by what it was hearing. The only laughs he got -- snickers, really, and unintended -- were the numerous malapropisms he kept dropping. They, unfortunately, came across loud and clear, as jarring notes often do.

All of a sudden, Bishop appeared to "get" it.

"Oh!" he said. "You mean, when what's-his-name, the guy who took the watch, turned out to be her brother . . . "

"Yes! Yes!" Silvers exclaimed. "See? Didn't I tell you it would all come out in the end?"

"I know, but . . . " Bishop hesitated. "I mean, if that's the case, what about --"

He stopped and shook his head, looking exceedingly unhappy.

Phil, simply unable to understand Joey's continued confusion, looked out at the studio audience, expecting to get their confirmation and appreciation. Alas, they were as in a painting, a still life, and gave him neither. All he saw was blank, uncomprehending faces staring back at him.

The wonderful comedian got that open-mouthed, querulous look on *his* face that he was well-known for on *Bilko*, which he would quickly snap out of on that show.

Not so here.

The silence in the studio was chilling.

Silvers turned to Joey and said, in a subdued voice, "I seem to have cast a pallor (sic) over the audience."

To close on yet another malapropism, particularly a doozy like that one, was, perversely, almost too good to be true.

"Listen, Phil," Bishop said, putting an end to it. "Thanks for coming. It was great seeing you." To the audience, he said: "Phil Silvers, ladies and gentlemen." (Applause, applause, applause.) And to the camera he declared, without any prompting:

"We'll be right back."

It was all terribly unfortunate.

But it did evoke a certain amount of awe, of the kind one experiences when witnessing a true disaster.

JOHNNY HAD COMPARABLE PROBLEMS WITH A few of his guests, as well.

There were two of them who absolutely froze on camera. Didn't -- couldn't -- make a sound.

Tuesday Weld was the first.

Backstage, the talented actress struck me as being oddly distant, even out of it. (She was not my assigned guest, but I couldn't keep my eyes off her.) There was also something about her behavior, as she kidded around with her agent, that just didn't look right to me.

When she made her entrance on the show, she had a fixed smile on her lovely face, and there it remained, throughout the foreshortened interview.

Never uttering a word.

Johnny handled it badly, though at first he made an effort to do the right thing. But, spurred by a few titters from the studio audience, he succumbed to temptation, rolling his eyes and rather pointedly running out of patience.

"Tuesday," he said, "do you understand what I'm saying? If you do, knock on the desk. Five times."

He demonstrated, bobbing his head on each count. Somebody made a whinnying sound. The audience laughed out loud . . . and that was the end of what little chance there was of Miss Weld coming around.

Art Stark was furious but showed it only by an impatient gesture towards the camera, which told Johnny to put an end to it, straightaway.

Carson went to commercial.

After the young actress exited, I can only assume she fled. Lord knows what must have been going through her mind.

On another occasion, the gifted Peter O'Toole was in the same fix.

He wasn't smiling, though, his expression one of extreme discomfort. He seemed dazed, actually. And, of course, terribly embarrassed.

Johnny handled O'Toole with great care. No comic asides, no sly remarks. Mercifully, he cut the interview short, with Art's blessing.

"We'll try again another time, Peter."

The actor nodded mutely, and left the set.

Johnny explained to the audience that O'Toole had just flown in from Tokyo and had had nothing to eat during the long flight. Drinking beer, and evidently lots of it.

Carson shrugged; these things happen.

I went backstage and on out into the corridor between studios 6A and 6B. There, O'Toole, fully cognizant of what had occurred, was in acute distress, talent coordinator, Bruce Cooper, doing his best to ease the actor's concerns.

Peter's wife, Sian Phillips, an actress herself, entered stage left. She was distraught, on the verge of tears. O'Toole tried to reassure her that everything was all right, luv, not to worry . . .

. . . and fell, as if pole-axed. Face down.

His wife dropped to the floor and gathered him up in her arms, making comforting sounds.

Remarkably, he was unhurt.

The actor wept.

Zsa-Zsa Gabor was nothing if not voluble. She said something she shouldn't have, one night, which we either missed outright or was of the kind we had become so inured to that we failed to pick up on its implications.

NBC did.

Fearing a potential lawsuit, they had it erased: several outrageously inappropriate remarks, with respect to a product she wasn't too crazy about.

At home, the TV audience saw Miss Gabor's lips moving, with nothing coming out. Some folks counted their blessings.

That, and Sinatra's earlier bad taste remark concerning Clifton Webb, were the only instances where audio cuts were ever deemed necessary.

Carson would have *liked* to edit the comic, Phil Foster.

He was from Brooklyn, still in the popular imagination a nesting ground for wild and crazy guys.

Phil did his best to live up to the stereotype. He snarled a lot, in what may have been mock-anger, but still apparently needed venting. A tough guy, his weapons of choice were random fulminations and sarcastic asides.

Foster's stories were often funny enough, but they never seemed to end. (Why should they? *Who's going to make me?*) As a consequence, they usually spilled over to the next segment, which meant they had to be recapitulated . . . and then, more of the same. What the man from Brooklyn didn't seem to realize was that this was not the *Phil Foster Show*.

I discussed the matter with the talent coordinator who worked with him, Shelly Schultz. He told me that, ironically, Foster was mad at *us*. And at the Associate Producer & Head Talent Coordinator, especially. At a meeting between him and me that he had requested, his first question was, "How come you don't like me?"

I explained that it wasn't a matter of my liking him or not liking him, and as best I could, went into what it *was* a question of.

Foster chuckled derisively, my analysis of the problem obviously striking him as the silliest thing he ever hoid (sic).

"Is that it?" he asked.

I nodded, stony.

Genuinely baffled, he said:

"I don't understand . . . "

"I know."

We looked at each other.

And that's where it ended.

So, you ask? Why did we keep using him?

Because not everyone agreed with me. And because, at any given moment, he may have been the only comic available.

With each of his appearances, we figured -- we hoped -- that *this* time he'd get the message.

He never failed to disappoint.

The comedian Jan Murray, a very nice fellow, had a similar problem, but for a different reason.

He told long stories -- momentum builders that depended on lots of repetition, and an unexpected finish. There was no way he could change his pattern to conform to the strictures of the talk show game. Unfortunately, audiences simply were not there for the extended tale -- for either Jan or Phil. Patience was not a virtue they were disposed to practice, when responding to those who took the lengthy route in seeking to amuse.

Jan did manage to tell, in a reasonably abbreviated form, about the time he was playing golf with Buddy Hackett and two other chums.

At one point, Buddy disappeared.

The players looked all over for him. Where was he? Hackett was nowhere to be found.

Suddenly, there he was, running out of the woods beyond the rough, naked as a jaybird, shouting:

"Locusts!"

ON ONE OF OUR SHOWS, AT AROUND TEN minutes to four, with taping scheduled for 6:30PM, as always, one of the guests fell out. Got ill, or something. It was the only time it ever happened -- a testimonial to how hardy people in the business are and how important it was for them to do the *Tonight Show*.

Our task, Art's and mine, was to come up with a replacement -- quick, fast and in a hurry.

I went to my list of generally available guests in and around New York City -- "B" players, for the most part. You don't call on celebrities to bail you out. (Talk about disrespect!)

Art shot down, out of hand, whatever name I brought up. I thought a little hesitation might have been in order. There was no guarantee, after all, that his choice would be available to us; and if he were, a pre-interview still had to be arranged and completed, over the phone. That would have to be processed, the result then dictated to Gloria Curry, my secretary. And distributed to Art and Johnny. *And* to the comedy writers.

The while, fighting the clock.

I came up with someone I thought would make a pretty good guest, particularly under the circumstances.

Stark shook his head.

"Too easy," he said.

Too easy?

What the hell was he talking about?

Another possible replacement came to mind, better but not by much than the guest Art had just rejected so cavalierly.

"That's the one!" he boomed, as if saying it emphatically would make it happen.

131

I called the responsible agent, who thought our guy might well be in town, he'd get right back to me.

He did, and he was.

I signified to Art that we were going to be all right, and called the new guest. It was now well past four o'clock, but stepping smartly, everything was pretty much wrapped up by a little before five.

Art's refusal to accept the first good name suggested to him, however, and his reason for doing so, have stayed with me all these years. The idea of resisting the expedient choice, digging instead a little deeper; of eschewing the facile solution -- both, "too easy" -- was something of an epiphany for me.

Whether or not I've always been able to live up to it is another story.

But let's not get too nutsy about this, okay?

ROD SERLING WAS NOT AT ALL THE GRAVE, unsmiling figure with the deep resonant voice most television viewers knew from seeing him hosting his own, landmark show, *The Twilight Zone*. Rod was warm and friendly, quick to laugh, and a boon to those of a creative bent. He was one of the good guys.

His flaw, which proved to be fatal, in my view, was that he bought into much of the nonsense of the 60s, particularly the mean-spirited, get-even notion that anyone over thirty had had it. Absurd on the face of it, but gospel to many, including some of those, themselves past the critical age, who should have known better. Look at the state of the world, the argument went. *Something* was wrong. Fractious young people accused their elders, all conveniently "over thirty," as being the ones at fault.

And, hence, no longer relevant.

The idea burrowed its way into Serling's psyche, reinforcing whatever feelings he may have had of diminished worth. He soon began to see himself as superannuated; for him, the party was ending, if not yet over.

He had been found out.

Actually, Rod was never a deep thinker. Merely a splendid storyteller -- *Patterns, Requiem For A Heavyweight*, and many, many more. Never fully realizing that the voice of the troubadour has its own resonance, the well-told tale a wondrous thing.

Rod died quite young -- in his early fifties, I believe. On the operating table. The word on the street in the medical community, with which I had a peripheral connection at the time, was that the operation -- a complicated but manageable heart procedure, even then; rather commonplace, today -- had been botched.

Some other good guys:

JAMES GARNER, certainly.

He always conveyed a reassuring sense of himself and his place in the universe. A grown up. Very congenial, though always holding something in reserve. A matter of upbringing and style, I would say. So different from my own background, not overly given to restraint. Noisier.

I quieted down, in Jim's company.

He was, in person, very much like the winning character he later played on *Rockford Files*.

Question: Which came first -- "Jimbo," or Garner to play him?

RICHARD CRENNA.
Another decent, straight-ahead guy. Bright and always . . . considerate. Yes, that's the word. A gentleman. He, too, often played -- plays -- mirror-image roles. Again, is it art drawing upon life, or the other way around?

I am attracted to certain actresses, whom I sometimes assume, unconsciously, are very much like the character they play on the screen. Maybe I'm not so crazy.

GEORGE SEGAL.
Blessed, or stuck, with a sweet nature and a sunny disposition. Inclined to smile and laugh a lot, both genuine.

Segal was one of the first, and few, actors of note who didn't change his Jewish-sounding surname. Not that it would have necessarily made him a bad person, had he done so.

I see George and Jim, were they to meet, getting along nicely, the one with characteristics not immediately evident in the other. And, after a while, walking away from it, before the bloom began to fade.

JOYCE BROTHERS, BLESS HER, WAS -- AND IS -- a wonderful woman, and still a friend, after all these years.

But something seems to happen to the good doctor when she is asked a question in her area of expertise. In responding, she tends to sound like she's calling the class to attention, slipping instantly into her lecture mode. (Her *voice* changes.) Everything about her says, this is *serious*.

Hell, that ain't her!

Joyce is fun. Lively. A delight to be with.

And I'm not just saying that because she laughs at practically all of my feeble attempts at humor.

SHARI LEWIS WAS A REMARKABLE ventriloquist, so skillful one hardly realized it wasn't the puppet who was doing the talking. That's what helped give her performances their air of credibility.

Lambchop, the gentle, little lamb, was the apotheosis of all her creations.

When she and I got together, coming up with things for her to talk about, as Shari, was never a problem. Author, star of her own children's television show, sometime symphony orchestra conductor, she lived a rich and varied life.

It was Lambchop's appearance that got all our attention. Finding a premise, suitable subject matter to talk about with Johnny. That *was* a problem. Something with bite to it. (Lambchop, with bite?) A point of view.

She and I would brainstorm, a relatively new concept at the time, in which one is not only given the license to come up with any suggestion, however outrageous, but is encouraged to do so. It was not as easy as it may sound, letting go of normal, social constraints. But we were good friends and got past the initial resistances soon enough.

Once we found the topic, Shari took over, devising just what Lambchop would say, at least enough of it to get the ball rolling between her -- Lambchop, that is -- and Johnny.

In Lewis's first segment, she talked about herself, for maybe four minutes, as planned, giving her more time in the next segment. Carson would usually close it out by inquiring about Shari's friend.

"Lambchop's fine, Johnny," Shari would say. "She's looking forward to seeing you."

"So am I," Carson would say, sounding like he meant it.

During the commercial, Lewis would move to the desk, sitting right next to Johnny, Lambchop at hand -- *on* her hand. Dick Carson came up on a tight, two-shot, the puppet only inches away from the host's face. Their exchanges went smoothly from the start, Lambchop talking a lot, rattling away, with Johnny mostly listening, as a father to a child. Genuinely involved, his superb comic instincts told him when *not* to be funny.

This could not be said of other comics she worked with, Shari told me, who were unable to keep from clowning around in a condescending manner towards the innocent puppet.

The studio audience was as still as children are, when totally absorbed.

The spot ran for a good eight minutes and could have gone on a hell of a lot longer.

A bit of magic.

Lambchop was Lewis's alter ego, or rather her quintessence: sweet, endlessly caring, childlike.

IT CAME TO PASS THAT, DURING ART AND Johnny's second, seven-week vacation period, I got to produce the *Tonight Show*.

(Applause, applause, applause.)

To cover their *first* summer hiatus, NBC, in its infinite wisdom, decided to give the other Associate Producer a crack at helming the show.

This came as a surprise to all of us on the seventh floor at 30 Rock.

The other Associate Producer -- hereinafter referred to as the OAP -- had been with the show since Steve Allen, *Tonight's* first host and its originator. Intelligent and accommodating, he was something of a mysterious figure, certainly from the time I first met him. Given, upon arriving mid-morning, to going straight to his office and closing the door behind him, there to stay, except for bathroom breaks (lunch was ordered in), and the two production meetings, at 12:15PM and 5:15PM, which everybody had to attend.

At those meetings, he behaved as if he was still an active member of the team (and was treated as such), when in fact he made only the smallest of contributions. Everyone knew that at some point he had lost his nerve, even as he maintained the fiction that he had not. None of us thought he'd be able to handle producing the show; all of us were committed to helping him as much as we could.

It never got that far.

For ten days, I had been after him to get together with me, and *start booking*. Jerry Lewis was coming in for the first two weeks, and we had only five guests up on the boards, covering both weeks -- booked prior to the OAP's ascendancy.

On the Friday before Jere was to start, I waited by my door, prepared to tackle him if necessary when he came in. (The OAP, not Jerry.) Our sworn-to, absolutely last-chance appointment was scheduled for 10:30AM.

At eleven o'clock, he appeared, hesitating before crossing the threshold. Head down, his face flushed, he whizzed by me and, once again, went straight into his office, closing the door behind him. A few minutes later, one of NBC's head honchos, long assumed to be the OAP's "rabbi" at the network -- neither of them Jewish -- arrived, moving fast, and joined him behind closed doors. Soon thereafter, a nurse showed up, pushing a wheelchair. By this time, all the other activity in the bullpen had ceased. We were as in a frieze, watching and waiting.

Finally, after what was actually only a few minutes, the OAP's door opened, and he was wheeled out by the nurse, the NBC executive trotting behind them. Eyes closed, head lolling to one side, the unfortunate fellow was on his way to the hospital. What had happened to him no one could be quite certain of. And when he came back, seven weeks later, on the day Stark returned, no one asked.

As soon as he left, I gathered up all of my lists and, together with the other talent coordinators, took over Art's office, at his suggestion. Somehow, by three o'clock, we managed to fill almost all the empty spots on both boards. When Jerry showed up, at around four-thirty, he was thrilled with what he saw.

The bookings consisted of many New York players -- "B" guests to us, but familiar names to Lewis, childhood heroes in some cases. Still stars, as far as he was concerned.

NBC hired an outside producer to take over.

For *this* summer, NBC made me and the OAP co-producers, giving him top billing.

I had mixed feelings about it, knowing I was going to have to do all the work, with the lines of authority between us not at all clearly defined, although nominally he would be in charge. Indeed, he sat in the producer's chair and presided over both production meetings, as if it was his rightful place.

That didn't sit well with me, especially when Ed McMahon, at every 5:15PM meeting -- evidently assuming the OAP *was* in charge -- bowed ceremoniously to him, palms pressed together in mock obeisance, saying, "Greetings, O Great White Father!" Very comical, to be sure, but it tended to reinforce the notion that the other guy was running the show.

I, in fact, had booked it, as I did all the others, for the full seven weeks. Routined it (as I did every show), determining the order in which the guests would appear, and for how long, plus any special pieces of business we might have had in mind. And handled my own guest, at the same time, while checking -- and absorbing -- what the other talent coordinators had come up with, for their guests. As well as working with each substitute host, making him feel as much at home as possible, and, before the taping, going over with him very carefully what was about to take place. The while, hopefully, making all the right moves *during* the taping.

Because I didn't want the OAP to feel completely left out, to be publicly embarrassed by my taking over every aspect of the game, I conveyed to him whatever decisions I made as we taped, which he then passed onto the booth.

That almost certainly meant that the director, Dick Carson, and the Associate Director, Bobby Quinn, assumed that it was he who made all those brilliant moves. Not me.

Nevertheless, I just loved it, producing the show, especially the taping part -- standing right next to Camera #1, directly in the guest host's line of sight. An encouraging nod, a smile when appropriate, just making eye contact, went a long way towards keeping an uncertain player on an even keel. And giving him, during the commercial breaks, whatever reassurances he may have needed, maybe even clowning around a little, and of course reminding him who and what was coming up…

In other words, dealing with the guest host as with the regular host, whoever he (or she) might be, only more so.

NBC was doubling my salary for the interim period, Dave Tebet told me, at the close of the first show. The word from on high. "Doubling" made it sound like a far bigger deal that it really was. From $225 to $450 a week. Another $225 a week, that is, to co-produce a show I was actually producing.

Yippee.

Most of the guest hosts lined up for a series of one-night stands, some hosting for as long as a week -- Sammy Davis, Jr., among them -- and in one instance, two-and-half weeks: Joey Bishop.

The one-nighters were a diverse group.

Country Western singing star, Eddy Arnold; comedian Allen Sherman ("Hello Muddah, Hello Faddah"); actor Donald O'Connor, who handled himself well. And Fat Jack E. Leonard, the original "insult" comic -- gentle, even soft-hearted, in person. A melange of players, lacking continuity, certainly, but kind of fun to watch over the short haul. Except for Arthur Godfrey, a former TV superstar -- for one season the biggest, actually, with *two* separate weekly half-hour shows, in prime time. A nasty piece of work, if there ever was one.

He was on CBS Radio when he hosted *Tonight*, his days of glory long since past.

Earlier that morning, at CBS, as a three-way conversation between him, me, and his producer, Peter Lasally, was winding down, Arthur left us to wrap things up, with the admonition, I've told you what to do, now go ahead and do it!

Apparently, we lingered too long.

He buzzed Lasally, who jumped a foot in the air, picking up the phone instantly and indicating after a beat that I should pick up, too.

"Are you guys still talking?" the ex-star wanted to know, emphasizing his incredulity. "What's the matter with you, for Christ's sake! I don't get it. It's not *that* hard, is it?"

He banged the telephone down.

Peter, sallow to begin with, paled even further.

I didn't envy him; it was a thoroughly gratuitous act of incivility on Godfrey's part. Evidently, Lasally survived it. Years later he became a key player in resolving the David Letterman/Jay Leno brouhaha, over who would succeed Carson as host of the *Tonight Show*, which he subsequently produced.

Not surprisingly, Godfrey was willful and uncooperative during the taping, the only one of the many guest hosts to pull that kind of crap. At one point, he steadfastly refused to take my repeated cue to go to commercial, no matter what I did, including straying onto the set (though outside of camera range), so he could "see" me. The network took it away from him, anyway, cutting him off in mid-sentence.

The look he gave me was venomous, as I approached the desk. Saying nothing, I merely pointed out to him who was coming up next, moved the guest Godfrey wouldn't give up on over to the couch, and returned to my station next to camera #1.

There, I lit up a cigarette and exhaled ostentatiously.

My stomach was roiling.

With Sammy Davis, Jr., I experienced a special moment of personal gratification, even as I wondered where the inspiration for it had come from.

On one of his shows, the guest I worked with directly was Phyllis Newman, married to Adolph Green, of Comden & Green. A very attractive, full-of-life gal, with a lovely smile, whom I was secretly kind of sweet on. (Now, it can be told.) She was an actress who sang, and also, I knew, did passable impressions of other singers -- chief among them, Judy Garland. Sammy, who we were all crazy about, used to do impressions too. His were dead-on. I figured it might be kind of fun to have a little spontaneous challenge between them. One that "just happened," with no elaborate set up. See where it might take us. In her second segment, Miss Newman would sing a song, in her own voice.

But with talk shows, even one so carefully planned as *our* talk show, the unexpected occasionally occurred.

Phyllis caught fire, doing her impressions as never before. Peaking on Judy Garland's "Over the Rainbow." Rising out of her chair, as if being levitated, when she hit the big closing notes.

"WHERE . . . OH, WHERE . . . AM . . . I?"

Now, fully standing, to thunderous applause.

On the instant, I realized her appearance had to end there, anything else beyond that moment certain to be anti-climactic.

Accordingly, I told the OAP to notify the booth that we were cutting Newman's song and bringing out the next guest, ahead of schedule -- actor Larry Blyden.

I turned towards Skitcher, who was bearing down on me. At the same moment that he said, "You're cutting her song, aren't you?" -- prepared to do battle, if I disagreed -- I was drawing a finger across my throat, saying precisely that. Over at the desk, I could see that Sammy was still blinded by the light.

I went up to him.

"Jesus!" he murmured, *sotto voce*. "I didn't know she was *that* good!"

"Neither did I."

I pointed to his notes on the next guest.

"Larry Blyden, coming up."

Phyllis heard me and left the swivel chair, moving to the couch. We exchanged smiles. She looked a trifle dazed.

When we came back from commercial, Sammy introduced Larry, and that was that.

But where had this flash of showbiz insight come from?

Perhaps I'm making too much of it.

No matter.

I LOVE THIS GAME!!

By the time we got to Joey Bishop, I had been at it for three or four weeks, and was no longer green. And he had guest-hosted before, so it went fairly smoothly.

When it didn't, Joey used it to his advantage, questioning me by name during the tapings. Asking me, ostensibly perplexed, if we were going to do such-and-such next, or what?

"Look at this," he'd say to the studio audience. "I ask him a question, and he lights up a cigarette and points to the camera -- meaning, I should go to commercial."

That's exactly what I meant. Whatever was bothering him, we'd discuss it during the break.

I pointed to the camera again.

(Laughter.)

Bishop was very good at that, and subsequently, on his own show, in one of its highlights, he would query his announcer, Regis Philbin, in a similar, banter-with-a-bite manner. It always worked.

There was another nice personal moment.

Talent coordinator, Shirley Wood, hesitatingly suggested during a commercial break that we might want to go to the story at the bottom of page two of her pre-interview with the guest of the moment.

I nodded and passed it along.

Her suggestion played nicely,   allowing us to exchange the kind of deeply satisfying, behind-the-scenes look that only professionals are privy to.

FOLLOWING MY STINT AT WHATEVER I HAD been with Bishop and the others, two of the top talent agencies in town came after me.   It was probably Joey's giving me a hard time that did it.

In my conversations with Bernie Weintraub and Sandy Gallin, at CMA (later, ICM), they brought up the distinct possibility, as they saw it, of my producing Joey Bishop's new talk show, which they had heard he was about to get at ABC.   They asked me how much I was presently making.   For the record, as it were.   When I told them, they both exploded in disbelief.

"Don't ever let *anyone* know that," they chorused. "Ever!"

My kind of guys.

"I mean it," Bernie reiterated, as I was leaving. "Tell no one."

EVIDENTLY, CARSON HAD HEARD THE WORD, as well.

His secretary, Jeannie Prior, called and asked if I could drop by, Johnny wanted to talk to me.

And talk he did.

"Sy, I hear you've been getting some offers . . . I don't want to lose you . . . Let me know if something happens, and I'll try to meet your price . . . I don't know if I'll be able to, with NBC, but I'll try."

It was the most direct exchange we'd ever had. He had been straightforward and *comfortable* with me, which I appreciated most of all. Well, after all this time . . .

I assured him I would.

A WEEK OR SO LATER, I GOT A CALL FROM BOB Williams, who wrote a daily column on TV for the New York Post. I had dozed off, while watching television, and was a little fuzzy when I answered.

Williams noted the Bishop possibility, as well as there being some talk about my producing Bill Dana's proposed new talk show, out of Las Vegas.

"Obviously, you're hot right now," he said, which I didn't quite catch.

"Pardon?"

"I said, 'Obviously, you're hot right now.'"

"Oh, yeah," I said. "I guess."

Scintillating.

The tale of my prospects made up the lead story in his column in the next day's Post. With my name spelled right, and everything.

THEN, BERNIE WEINTRAUB, MY NEW AGENT, called.

"Feel like taking a trip?"

He ticked off the airline, flight number, date and time, and told me to write them down.

"Joey wants to fly you out to L.A. this weekend. First class. All very hush-hush. You'll be back late Sunday afternoon."

(Bishop must have heard the talk, too.)

"Can you make it?" Bernie asked.

"I'll be there with bells on, " I replied. "I'll look silly, but I'll wear 'em, anyway."

"Good," he said.

It was my first time in First Class, so already I was ahead of the game.

Sitting a few rows in front of me, and to my right, was a woman of surpassing beauty. Someone the womenfolk in my family would have called "stunning." Faye Dunaway. She had just won an Obie, for best performance by an actress in an off-Broadway play, *Hogan's Goat*. On her way to the Coast, probably to test the waters.

At one point, she gave me a sidelong glance from under her picture hat.

Now, I was really ahead of the game.

Bishop picked me up in his brand new Silver Cloud Rolls Royce. Bernie was there, too, and I believe Joey's brother, a quiet fellow, who did the driving.

Over the weekend, in the only conversation Joey and I had with any meat on it, he said, "I don't know, Sy. I haven't heard anything new, yet . . . " I told him I was still getting used to the idea of producing his show and didn't have anything 'new' in mind.

"I can promise you this," I said. "You'll have the best production you could possibly ask for. Top quality guests, all professionally handled. A smoothly oiled machine."

I took a sip of my drink.

"Whatever coloration the show takes on, Joey, will come from you, anyway. The special thing you bring to it. There's nothing *new* in this business. You know that. It's the *way* you do it. *That's* what counts."

He nodded, evidently satisfied with my answer, as far as I could tell.

I realized later that I had been drawing unconsciously upon an impromptu jousting that had once taken place between him and Milton Berle, when Berle had complained that Bishop was doing all his material.

"Timing and delivery make the difference," Joey pointed out, artfully.

BACK WITH THE SHOW, I PRE-INTERVIEWED Elia Kazan, the well-known director, in motion pictures and the theater -- *On The Waterfront*, *Streetcar* . . . -- who had written a novel, *The Arrangement*. I told him I had spotted someone on the Coast who I thought might make a wonderful wife to the book's hero, in the movie version. A fresh face.

"Thanks" Kazan said, "but I've already chosen the actress to play her -- my girlfriend, Barbara Loden."

The film came out two years later. It starred Kirk Douglas and -- trumpets flourish! -- Faye Dunaway.

BERNIE CALLED AGAIN. THE BISHOP SHOW was a mortal lock, he stated unequivocally. Be patient. These things take time.

I told him not to worry.

"I'm not going anywhere."

THERE WAS AN AFTRA STRIKE GOING ON. THE American Federation of Television & Radio Artists. None of us had paid much attention to it, the issues involved obscure and peripheral, and we were, you know -- busy. Until Carson decided to honor it, as part of some kind of arcane negotiating ploy against NBC. He called us off the show, for reasons we knew not why. It was an unanticipated vacation, shrouded in uncertainty, and none of us were happy about it.

The only thing we knew *with* certainty was that, during this period, NBC had hired a substitute staff, with guest hosts, the producer, Perry Cross. The guy taking my place, occupying my office -- too freeking small, but mine own -- was being paid $750 a week!

When we did find out what was going on behind the scenes, it was a shocker: Art Stark was out, as producer of the *Tonight Show*!!

He came over to my place for a cup of coffee, so angry "he couldn't see straight," his rage, his humiliation, carrying him. He said he felt betrayed. I commiserated with him. Between the two of us, there was a whole lot of head-shaking going on.

Later, thinking it over, it occurred to me that, in fact, Art had failed to accommodate himself to the change in Johnny's status. Carson was now an authentic star, no longer the producer's protégé. The way things had been between them just wouldn't play anymore.

Then, ignoble thoughts assailed me.

Who would be taking his place? And could it be little ol' me?

Shame, shame, shame: dancing on the grave of a good friend.

Fortunately, such speculation ceased altogether, when I got a call from a well-connected fellow worker, who told me I was out, too.

Well, naturally. Of course. I mean, Art and I were a tandem. If he went, I had to go, as well.

The next day, Johnny called me.

"May I speak to Sy Kasoff, please?"

"It's me, Johnny," I told him. Who the hell did he *think* he was talking to?

"Oh, Sy . . . " he said. He cleared his throat. "Sy, I've been thinking of making some changes . . . "

"That's okay, Johnny," I said. "I heard."

"Thanks, pappy," he said, and hung up. "Pappy" was what I had been calling some of the guys, lately, Lord knows why. It was silly. Ridiculous.

Thanks, pappy!

Not that any of it really mattered. I had a 'mortal lock' on ABC's newly announced official entry into late night, *The Joey Bishop Show*. I would be leaving the *Tonight Show* soon anyway.

But, the next day, Bernie called. He told me the deal just fell through. Joey had changed his mind the last minute, no one knew why. Weintraub said he was truly sorry.

Six months later, Ed Hookstratten, an important player in the business and an advisor to Bishop, let me in on what had happened. At the last minute, Jack Paar had called Joey and asked him, as a personal favor, to give the job to the guy who used to produce his show and hadn't worked since Jack had left it -- maybe five years earlier.

Bishop, who received his first national exposure as a guest of Paar's and felt obligated to him, said okay.

Curses! Foiled by Jewish sentimentality!

Those New York comics were full of it.

TWO YEARS PASSED.

I was now in L.A., moving along, singing a song. You can't keep a good man down, and you can't keep me down, either.

Milt DeLugg called. He had succeeded Skitch Henderson as leader of *The Tonight Show* orchestra and was in town to do a Carson special.

"Meet me at NBC Burbank, and we'll do lunch around here."

I told him I felt a little uneasy about coming there, not having seen or talked to Johnny since he bade me farewell over the phone. At Milt's urging, I shrugged it off and agreed to join him.

When I entered Studio 6A, Carson was off in the distance, rehearsing a drum solo -- looking as uncomfortable as I felt.

After he finished, he headed towards a group of guys standing, as it happened, just a few feet in front of me.

Upon joining them, a remarkable thing occurred.

He looked right at me . . . but only for a nano-second, his eyes sweeping away, only to return a moment later; then sweeping away again. Then, returning, and away, over and over, his gaze never coming to a full stop. Making eye contact, if you can call it that, but just for a fraction of an instant.

It was true that since we had parted company, I had

grown a moustache, but otherwise I was wholly recognizable. Johnny recognized me, there's no doubt in my mind.

Meanwhile, I was struggling to keep up with his frenetic eyeballing, the expression on my face purposefully benign, bright with welcome. Thinking, *stop doing that, please!*

At that point, Milt hailed me, and I turned away to join him. We headed out the door. I was, I admit it, thoroughly shaken.

It seems Johnny and I had come full circle.

He was uncomfortable with me (and everyone else) when we met . . . and he was *still* uncomfortable with me now.

After all this time.

FINAL THOUGHTS

The four-and-a-half years I spent on the *Tonight Show* have, it seems, pretty much stayed with me all these years. Thus, the near-total recall.

In writing about it, I did not have a day-by-day chronology in mind. Rather, I wanted to put together the bits and pieces my memory dished up into a kind of mosaic -- more a pastiche, actually -- that hopefully would capture, at least in part, the ambience, the *flavor* of the period. And its vicissitudes. An impressionistic piece, roughly paralleling the random, wayward nature of the journey, itself.

But in trying to capture the emotions I experienced at the time, some of them inevitably bubbled up and spilled over, making it appear that I still felt about Johnny as I did then. Particularly considering how I've made no bones about my unhappiness with NBC, *to this day*, over the slave wages they paid the talent coordinators . . . and the size of my office, dammit.

However, as to my feelings for the host of the show presently , it just isn't so.

A woman I know said to me, after reading portions of my manuscript, "Oh, my. You're very angry with Johnny, aren't you? I mean, *right this minute* . . . "

Really? Naw! Uh-uh.

Was I ever angry with Carson during those days?

Absolutely.

It is not uncommon for the staff of a show to have moments of distemper towards the person they soldier for, even as they revel in the relationship, bask in its reflected glory. To be in thrall to another person is to invite resentment, with anger all too often in its wake.

But am I angry *now*?

Certainly, not.

In point of fact, my feelings towards Johnny became more and more sanguine, as the writing progressed. That's what prompted me to cite specific instances of his okay behavior. The way he dealt with the Maharishi Mahesh Yogi and Salvador Dali -- all too easy targets, had he opted to go after them. And the colossal restraint he displayed with Murray Roman, endlessly at his ear, until just before show time.

How great he was with Lambchop . . .

One thing is indisputable.

Johnny was a considerably more complicated figure than everyone had generally assumed him to be.

And so were my feelings about him, as I had assumed *them* to be.

I wonder how he would react to the book.

Maybe, I'll send him a copy.

What the hey!

ABOUT THE AUTHOR

For many years I was a writer/producer in television, concentrating in the beginning on talk shows . . .

I started on the *Tonight Show* as a talent coordinator; soon became Head Talent Coordinator; and then, Associate Producer & Head Talent Coordinator. (NBC was long on titles, short on bread.) And I produced the show in the summertime.

Following the *Tonight Show*, I produced a special six-hour, talk show/fundraiser, hosted by Jack Paar, in Washington, D.C. It was for Ethel and Bobby Kennedy, for the benefit of their favorite charity, "Junior Village."

Subsequently I produced three syndicated talk shows, out of L.A.: *Pat Boone In Hollywood*, *The Ed Nelson Show* and *The His & Her Of It*.

I now live a quiet life (too quiet) in my hometown of Providence, R.I.

Printed in the United States
25582LVS00002B/1-15